Reluctantly Alice

BOOKS BY PHYLLIS REYNOLDS NAYLOR

Witch's Sister
Witch Water
The Witch Herself
Walking Through the Dark
How I Came to Be a Writer
How Lazy Can You Get?
Eddie, Incorporated
All Because I'm Older
Shadows on the Wall
Faces in the Water
Footprints at the Window
The Boy with the Helium Head
A String of Chances
The Solomon System
The Mad Gasser of Bessledorf Street
Night Cry
Old Sadie and the Christmas Bear
The Dark of the Tunnel
The Agony of Alice
The Keeper
The Bodies in the Bessledorf Hotel
The Year of the Gopher
Beetles, Lightly Toasted
Maudie in the Middle
One of the Third Grade Thonkers
Alice in Rapture, Sort of
Keeping a Christmas Secret
Bernie and the Bessledorf Ghost
Send No Blessings
Reluctantly Alice

Reluctantly Alice

Phyllis Reynolds Naylor

ALADDIN PAPERBACKS
New York London Toronto Sydney Singapore

First Aladdin Paperbacks edition June 2000

Aladdin Paperbacks
An imprint of Simon & Schuster
Children's Publishing Division
1230 Avenue of the Americas
New York, NY 10020

10 9 8 7

The Library of Congress has cataloged the hardcover edition as follows
Naylor, Phyllis Reynolds
Reluctantly Alice / Phyllis Reynolds Naylor—1st ed
p   cm
"A Jean Karl book "
Summary Alice experiences the joys and embarrassments of seventh grade
while advising her father and older brother on their love lives
ISBN 0-689-31681-X (hc)
[1 Schools—Fiction 2 Single-parent family—Fiction 3 Family life—Fiction] I Title
PZ7 N24Re   1991
[Fic]—dc20   90-37956 CIP AC
ISBN 0-689-81688-X (Aladdin pbk)

To Catherine Wood, my college speech teacher,
who generously considered my writings entertaining,
and to Marion Tucker, an early editor,
who helped make them better

CONTENTS

1 ❀ *The Seventh Thing*

IN SEVENTH grade, you grow backwards. In sixth, I kept a list of all the things I learned that showed I was growing up, and another of all the stupid, embarrassing things I did that proved I wasn't. Most of the time they were about even. If I still kept a record of all I've done, my "backwards" list would run right off the page. In a single day—the first day of seventh grade—I accidentally squirted a teacher at the drinking fountain, tripped on the stairs to the second floor, and sat on a doughnut in the cafeteria.

"Who put a doughnut on this seat?" I asked the girl next to me.

"It's for Kim," she said.

Now what kind of an answer was that? But even Patrick laughed when it happened.

"Well, how are you liking junior high, Al?" Dad asked that night while we were fixing dinner. My name is Alice, but he and Lester call me "Al."

"Ask me tomorrow," I said. "Ask me next week."

"That bad, huh?" said Lester. Lester's almost twenty and catches on quick.

"I can think of at least seven things about seventh grade that stink," I told him. "The boys are shorter than the girls, the math is too hard, Mr. Hensley has bad breath, there isn't any toilet paper in the johns, we're going to cook liver in home ec., and half the drinking fountains don't work."

"That's only six," said Dad.

"The cafeteria serves garbage."

"You could always transfer back to sixth," Lester suggested, tackling his salad.

"Ha, ha," I said. "And don't take all the Bacon Bits. We live here, too."

I'd been thinking about sixth grade, though—my sixth-grade teacher, anyway, Mrs. Plotkin. Sometimes when I get upset—*really* upset—I sort of tell myself what I figure she'd say if she were there. Stuff like, "Well, Alice, there aren't many perfect days, but it's hard to find a day that doesn't have a *little* something nice about it if you look." It helped, somehow—just saying words like that aloud and pretending it was her voice, not mine.

Dad and Mrs. Plotkin must be on the same wavelength, because just then he said, "Think of at least one good thing about seventh grade. Surely there's *one.*"

"We get out at two-thirty instead of three."

"So there you are," said Dad.

I guess the main problem is that seventh grade's so different from elementary that it takes some getting used to. Pamela Jones likes it. All Pamela talks about is what she's going to wear to the eighth-grade dances, and seventh's one step closer than sixth. When you've got blond hair so long you can sit on it, I guess you can expect to get asked to a lot of dances.

Elizabeth Price hates junior high, though—the way people swarm at you in the halls. She was going to switch to the Sacred Heart of the Blessed Mary Middle School but found out they don't have curtains on their shower stalls, so she reconsidered.

"I'll probably get used to it after a while," I said as I passed the macaroni and stopped Lester from taking all the cheese on top. "I remember I had a hard time in kindergarten too, but I got over it."

"You did, Al?" asked Dad.

I couldn't help smiling. "There was this boy who made faces at me from behind an easel—he was painting on one side and I was on the other. Every day he'd make faces and I'd cry. Then Mom told me that next time he poked his face around the easel, I should paint a stripe on it, so I did."

Lester laughed, but Dad went on chewing. "That must have been Aunt Sally who told you that, Al, because your mother died just before you started kindergarten."

I always manage to do this—confuse Mom with Aunt Sally, and it freaks Dad out.

"Sorry," I said. "Anyway, it worked. The next time the boy made a face at me, I painted a black stripe on his forehead. He stuck out his tongue, so I painted that too. He never bothered me again."

"Good old Aunt Sally," said Les.

What's really worst about being in seventh grade is that you just got out of sixth. In sixth grade, you're a safety patrol. You get to go on overnight field trips with your teachers, help out in the office, and rule the playground. If two people form a couple, then everyone pairs off, and the fourth and fifth graders are green with envy.

But when you start seventh grade, you're at the bottom of the ladder again. You look weird. You feel weird. The boys and girls who were couples back in sixth grade pretend they don't know each other anymore. I mean, when Patrick and I kissed last summer, it was a quick kiss with his hands on my shoulders, and then we edged over to our own sides of the glider again.

When couples kiss in eighth and ninth grades, I discovered, they touch their lips together lightly two or three times first, and then it's so embarrassing you have to look away. If their bodies were any closer, they'd be a grilled cheese sandwich.

Almost everything that Pamela Jones told us about seventh grade, that her cousin in New Jersey told *her*, was wrong. So far, anyway. You don't have to have a boyfriend or a leather skirt, either one. What you worry about, instead, is whether you can remember your coat locker and P.E. locker combinations both, whether you can get from one end of the building to the other before the bell, whether you'll drop your tray in the cafeteria and everyone will clap, and whether, when you go in the rest room, there will be any latches on the stalls.

It didn't help, either, that I had started junior high with an allergy. Dad says that happens sometimes when you move from one part of the country to another. I'd been doing a lot of sneezing the last couple of years, but the fall of seventh grade was absolutely the worst. I had to have Kleenex with me all the time at school, and the large girl who sat in front of me in Language Arts was always looking over her shoulder whenever I blew my nose.

I don't know what it was, though—maybe the Sara Lee brownies we had for dessert—but after telling Dad the one good thing I could think of about seventh grade, I felt better, and realized that at this particular time in my life, I was friends with everybody. I'll admit that seventh grade was only one day old, but suddenly I had this new goal: to go the whole year with everyone liking me. I don't mean be "most popular girl" or anything; I just wanted teachers to smile when they said "Alice McKinley" and the other kids to say, "Alice? Yeah, she's okay. She's neat."

Alice the Likable, that would be me. So there were at least two good things now about seventh grade: We got out earlier, and I was starting a brand new school, friends with everyone so far, even Patrick.

By Wednesday of the first week, the count of good things about seventh grade had gone up to three: no recess in junior high. I didn't realize how much I hated recess until there wasn't any. You didn't *have* to put on your coat and go stand out in the cold. You didn't *have* to play tag ball whether you wanted to or not. You didn't have a teacher blowing a whistle at you every fifteen seconds, or have third-grade boys trying to hit you with volley balls. There was P.E., of course, but what you got instead of recess was an extra long lunch hour, and you could do anything you wanted.

By Thursday morning, I had numbers four and five: In seventh grade, you're only in class with a certain teacher for forty minutes, so if it turns out to be someone awful, you don't have to stand it all day. The other thing is that the school has its own newspaper—the students write it themselves—and it's a lot more interesting than the newsletter we put out in sixth grade.

The sixth good thing about seventh grade—absolutely astounding—I discovered Thursday afternoon in P.E. It was the first day we had actually undressed and put on our gym shorts and T-shirts. The class was made up of some seventh-, eighth-, and ninth-grade girls together, and though the shower stalls had curtains on them and each of us had a towel to wrap up in when we stepped out, some of the older girls didn't wrap.

Seventh-grade girls used their towels like aluminum

foil, encircling their bodies and sealing the seams, but some of the older girls stepped out of the showers, their towels around their hair instead, with their entire bodies on view for the rest of us, the seventh graders in particular.

For the first time in my whole twelve years, I saw naked breasts—big breasts—in person. I couldn't help staring, they were just so amazing. They came in all shapes and sizes and some were huge. I mean, compared to the breasts I saw in P.E., Pamela, Elizabeth, and I hadn't even sprouted yet. We were still buds on a tree, moths in a cocoon, tadpoles in a pond, mosquitoes in eggs.

I talked about it at dinner that night, and for once I had Lester's full attention. When I'd finished my revelations about the wonders of the female breast, Dad gave me a little smile and said, "Your mother did nurse you, you know. You're not quite as deprived as you think."

"A lot of good that did me. I was too young to remember."

"And you never saw your Aunt Sally's breasts?" Dad asked.

I stared. "Are you kidding? Aunt Sally wears vinyl siding for a bathrobe!" (She doesn't, of course. The times we've visited her in Chicago, she's worn a chenille robe, but she clutches it closed with two hands.)

"What about Carol?" Lester asked. Carol is Aunt Sally's daughter, and she's a couple years older than Les. "You never saw her in the nude?"

"No," I said. "Did you?"

Lester turned bright red.

"*Got*-cha!" I said.

"No," Lester said quickly. "I never did. Don't be stupid."

"Well, then!" said Dad. "You've achieved a twelve-year goal today, Al! So how are you liking seventh grade?"

"Fine," I told him. "And if I can think of one more good thing about it, it'll cancel out all the bad ones."

I went to school on Friday searching for it—the seventh good thing about seventh. I wanted to like junior high. According to Mrs. Plotkin, *wanting* to do things is half the battle. In each of my classes I looked for something that was different from sixth grade that made junior high better. The teacher in Life Science was nice. So was Miss Summers in Language Arts. Nice and pretty, too. My math instructor was kind and was good at explaining problems, but as the day went on and I was in and out of classrooms, there wasn't one particular class that stood out. Finally there was just one period left, Mr. Hensley's World Studies, and I thought, "Wouldn't it be great if I discovered the Seventh Wonder of Seventh Grade in here?"

This is the only class I have with Patrick, and all week we'd been sitting in the last row, as far as we could get from Mr. Hensley's bad breath. Patrick hasn't exactly been ignoring me, but after we'd seen the way eighth and ninth graders make out at lunch time, leaning against the walls outside, all the kids who had been going together as couples in sixth grade sort of developed amnesia. None of us wanted to remember the silly things we'd done over the summer. Like the boys running around the playground with Pamela's new Up-Lift, Spandex, Ahh-Bra. No ninth-grade boy would do that, and no ninth-grade girl would get hysterical if he did. So here before class is the one place Patrick and I can talk a little and catch up on things without attracting attention.

"How's it going?" Patrick said.

"Better. I actually think I'm going to like junior high." I crossed my fingers. "Maybe." I stole him a look. "You been to P.E. yet?" I wondered if seventh-grade boys had the same kind of revelations when they looked at older boys in the nude as girls did when they saw older girls in the shower.

"Yeah! It's neat!" Patrick said. "We're doing track right now, and you should see the legs on some of those guys on our team!"

I smiled.

Then the bell rang and Horse-Breath Hensley was up in front of the room, pacing back and forth the way he does when he talks to the class. This time he was talking about fairness, and the way he was going to conduct the class. He'd already given us an outline of the course and told us when the big reports were due, and he said that he knew he wasn't one of the most exciting teachers in the school, but he hoped we would remember him as one of the fairest. So far so good, I thought. Maybe this will be the Seventh Thing.

Then Mr. Hensley said that probably all our lives, we had been treated alphabetically as an example of fairness. The Adamsons were always called on first in class and the Zlotskys were always called on last.

True, I thought, but I'll admit I'd always liked that. With a last name right smack in the middle of the alphabet, it had always been comforting to know that I wouldn't be the first to have to stand up and give a report or the last one, either. If Mr. Hensley reversed it and called on the Z's first and the A's last, "McKinley" would still be in the middle. I smiled to myself.

"And so," Mr. Hensley said, "just to even things up a bit, in this class we go alphabetically by *first* names, and we're seated accordingly. If you will now move to the desks I assign/you. . . . Alice McKinley, first seat, first row, please. Barbara Engstrom, next seat, first row . . ." He read off his list, filling up the front row all the way across, then starting on the second.

I don't remember the rest. The only thing I knew for certain was that the class was rearranged, Patrick and I were separated, and I realized that for the rest of the semester I would be the first one called on for everything. I was also directly in line of fire of Mr. Hensley's breath.

"I think that was a *wonderful* idea!" said a girl named Yvonne Allison as we left the room.

I swallowed. The seventh best thing about seventh grade turned out to be the worst of all.

2 ❀ *Helping Lester*

IT WAS Lester, though, who was having real trouble at the moment. Lester turned twenty that Friday. He had just transferred from Montgomery College to the University of Maryland for his junior year, but was working part-time at Maytag, so Dad and I waited till he got home to have his celebration. The problem was that two girls had sent him presents, and Lester had to tell one of them that it was over. I'd never seen him so miserable.

"Lester," I said, after he'd opened my present, which was two half-pound bars of Hershey's chocolate, light and dark, with and without almonds. Dad had gone out in the kitchen for the ice cream. "Why do you have to give one girl up? Why can't you keep one as your true love and the other as best friend or something?"

"Don't be stupid," said Les. Then he remembered I'd just given him the chocolate, so he tried to explain: "I always thought it was the real thing with Marilyn, Al. And then, when she broke it off and I finally met Crystal, I figured maybe it was for the best, because I really like Crystal. Now that Marilyn wants me back, I realize how much I love her, but I can't seem to make myself give up Crystal. And neither one of them would settle for being only 'best friend.' Take my word for it."

Boy, I'd never had anything like that happen to me, and I was glad I wasn't in Lester's shoes. "Crystal doesn't even know yet?"

"She knows I heard from Marilyn. She knows I'm thinking it over. But she thinks she still has a chance."

"And she doesn't?" I studied my brother—the way his mustache sort of drooped at the corners. Lester's mustache makes him look a lot older than he is.

Lester shook his head. "It's Marilyn. I know it's Marilyn. I've never loved anyone in my life as much as Marilyn."

"What if you give up Crystal and then Marilyn dumps you again?" I asked.

"I'll kill her," said Lester.

Dad came in with the ice cream and a Pepperidge Farm chocolate layer cake. "You know what I think?" he said. "I think you're too young, too fast, and too far, Lester. You really ought to consider cooling it with both girls for six months or so, and see how you feel then."

"Get real," said Lester.

I wondered which girl I would like most to have for a sister-in-law. Marilyn plays the guitar; Crystal plays the clarinet. Marilyn is slender, with long brown hair. Crystal has short red hair and huge breasts. Both treat me really nice. If I was a bridesmaid for Marilyn, we'd probably be outdoors in a field, barefoot, in white cotton dresses. If I was a bridesmaid for Crystal, the wedding would be in a cathedral with music by Bach. I can't sing, but I know enough about music to know that if it's Crystal Harkins, the music will be Bach. I couldn't decide which girl to choose, either.

"Why don't you just let fate decide it?" I said, swishing some fudge ripple ice cream around in my mouth. "Whichever girl's birthday is nearest your own, marry her."

"If you can't say something intelligent, Al, just shut up," Lester told me, and I realized that Dad and I weren't any more help to him right then than he and Dad are to me sometimes. A lot of the time. *Most* of the time, in fact. What I need most of all in my life is the one thing I haven't got: a mother.

If I'd had a mother when I sat on a jelly doughnut the first day of school, she would have known what to say when I told her about it. When I told Pamela and Elizabeth, they each said, "I'd simply die!" When I told Lester, he just laughed. When I told Dad, he got logical and asked what the doughnut was doing on the seat in the first place, and how it should have been on the table. It didn't *matter* why the doughnut was on the seat. What mattered was that it *was*, and I sat on it.

A mother, I think, would have listened and agreed that it was embarrassing, but not the end of the world. She would have come up with something snappy to say if that, or anything like it, ever happened again. And most of all, she would have explained how to wash jelly off the seat of my pants without making it look as though I'd wet my jeans.

If I had to sit on that jelly doughnut again or be Lester right now, I wasn't sure which I'd choose. In any case, the phone rang, so I went out in the hall to answer. It was Marilyn.

"Hi, Alice," she said, and her voice was like wind chimes, tinkly, high and sweet. I remembered how she'd come to dinner once in a long skirt and I'd wanted to be like her so I went upstairs and put on a nightgown with a blouse over it and she hadn't even laughed. I really liked Marilyn and wondered if there was anything I could say that would help Lester.

"It's been a long time since I talked to you, Marilyn," I said.

"I know. Too long. Much too long. Is Lester enjoying his birthday? I know he probably just got home, but I wondered if he'd opened my present yet."

"He probably opened it in private," I told her, then realized how dumb that sounded—as though her gift was probably so personal he wouldn't have dared open it in front of the family. "I mean, Lester isn't real big on presents anymore. What I mean is ..."

"It's okay, Alice," Marilyn said quietly, but I thought she sounded hurt.

"No, what I *mean* is ..."

"You don't have to explain."

"He loves *you* best!" I blurted out.

There was silence at the other end of the line. "Best of *who*?" she asked finally. And suddenly I realized that while Crystal knew about Marilyn, Marilyn probably didn't know about Crystal.

"A-anybody," I said. "Me or Dad or *anybody*!"

"Oh," said Marilyn.

Lester came out of the kitchen. "Is that Marilyn?" he asked.

"Here's Lester!" I said quickly, and handed the phone to him.

I don't know how one person can get in as much trouble as I do. Things would have been okay, I guess, if Crystal hadn't called next. By then, Lester had the stereo going so loud he didn't even hear the phone ring, so I got it on the upstairs extension just as I was eating graham crackers before bed.

"Hi, Alice," Crystal said, and it sounded as though she'd been crying. "Did Lester have a nice birthday?"

"Yeah, a really great birthday," I said, wishing that Les, not me, had answered. And when Crystal didn't say anything else, I added, "He got presents from Dad and me and you and ... from Dad and me and you."

I heard Crystal swallow.

"Do you want me to get Lester?" I asked.

"No," Crystal said, and blew her nose. Now I knew

for sure she was crying. "I—I just wondered if he'd opened my gift yet. I guess I thought he'd call."

I couldn't stand the idea of Crystal crying. I was thinking about the time last summer I'd got a permanent, and my hair was all smelly and the curls were as tight as corkscrews. I was crying, and Crystal had come upstairs and made me beautiful. She'd shown me how to blow-dry my hair to make the curls large and wavy. Except for Mrs. Plotkin, I don't think I'd ever loved a female person as much in my life as I had loved Crystal then, unless it was Mama, long ago, whom I hardly remember.

"I shouldn't have c-called," Crystal wept. "It's just so hard, Alice."

"Oh, Crystal!" I said. "Lester really does like you."

" 'Like' isn't enough," Crystal said, and cried some more.

I was desperate. "He said he just can't give you up."

Crystal stopped crying. "He *did*?"

I gulped. "I heard him say it. He said, 'I just can't give her up.' "

"Are you sure it was *me* he was talking about?"

"Y-yes."

"Oh, Alice, you don't know how happy you've made me."

"Just a minute! I'll go get Lester," I said quickly.

"No, no! *Please* don't get him. Don't even tell him I called. You told me all I needed to know," Crystal said. "G'night, love." She made a kissing sound over the phone and hung up.

I felt terrible. I felt awful. I couldn't stand it. I marched across the hall and opened Lester's door.

"You stink!" I yelled.

Lester turned down his stereo. "What?"

And then I remembered it was his birthday. "Happy birthday," I said.

"Oh," said Lester, and turned the volume up again.

The next day, Saturday, Lester went to work at Maytag, and I went to the Melody Inn, the music store, where Dad's the manager. I work there three hours every Saturday, helping out wherever Dad needs. On the way there, I was thinking how—when I left school on Friday—I'd thought I had the worst problems in the family because I was in the first seat in the front row in history class, and how when I went to bed Friday night, I figured that Lester had a lot worse problems than I had. By the time I was through working my three hours at the Melody Inn, though, I knew it was Dad who had the most trouble of all.

There are two women who work at the Melody Inn —Janice Sherman, the assistant manager, who takes care of the sheet music department, and Loretta Jenkins, who runs the Gift Shoppe at the back of the store. Loretta chews gum and has wild curly hair, while Janice Sherman looks and acts like a lady banker. She dresses in suits and scarves and has a smile that stretches just so far and no farther. She's also had a crush on my dad ever since we moved to Maryland, I think, and I'm not sure Dad knows it.

The worst part, though, is that she let us use her

beach cottage at Ocean City for a week in August because I think she thought it would help Dad fall in love with her, even though she was back in Silver Spring minding the store. Instead, Dad fell for the lady in the beach house next to hers. And when I walked into the Melody Inn on this particular Saturday in early September, I had the feeling that somehow Janice had found out. I was assigned to help her in sheet music, and I happened to notice that she wasn't smiling at all. Her lips didn't even stretch.

"Check in this order, Alice," she said, "and make sure that we got all five copies of Chopin's *Mazurkas*, eleven copies of Bach's *Preludes*, and all the single titles listed on this sheet. If they check out, then copy the prices on these stickers and put one on each piece of music."

"Okay," I told her, and waited for her to say, "How's school going?" or "How are things at your house?" or any of the other things she usually says to me on Saturdays. She didn't.

Here were Dad and Lester each involved in woman troubles. I began to feel really lucky that Patrick and I were back to just being friends again, and I didn't have to worry about who to love first or best or most. Dad's problem, though, was that he didn't even know he had one. As far as Dad was concerned, Janice was just his assistant manager whom he took to concerts once in a while, but as far as Janice was concerned—I could see it in her eyes—she wanted to end up Mrs.

Ben McKinley some day, only she never told Dad about it and he never guessed.

It's really awkward when you know something's wrong, but you can't talk about it. Janice Sherman was nice to me; she was just awfully quiet, as though her thoughts were a million miles away. Well, a hundred and fifty miles, anyway: Ocean City, Maryland. So after I got all the sheet music checked in and a price sticker on everything and the music filed away in the drawer, I said, "It was really nice of you to let us use your beach cottage, Janice. We all had a really great time."

"Apparently so," said Janice, sort of sadly, I thought.

I knew I'd done it again. I considered putting a Band-Aid over my mouth to keep it shut until Monday morning so I couldn't do any more damage than I already had. But then I discovered that I could get in just as much trouble not saying anything at all. Because just before I went home at noon, Janice said, "Well, I'm glad your family could use my cottage, Alice. It's a shame to let it sit there empty when someone could be enjoying it. Did you have any visitors?"

All sorts of alarms went off in my head, and I knew I'd have to be careful. I knew right away that she wondered if the woman next door had come over. The woman had, as a matter of fact, but she and Dad had stayed out on the front porch talking. She never came in.

"The only people we had overnight were friends of mine," I told her.

"Well, sometimes it's nice just to have people in for dinner," Janice said.

"Nope, just my friends," I said, glad I could be honest. I sort of edged toward the door.

"Oh, what a shame!" said Janice. "What did your dad do all week? Swim a lot?"

"No, he doesn't swim much," I said. "Mostly he just read and listened to music and stuff." I knew it was the "and stuff" that bothered her.

"Just kept to himself with all those people around?" Janice kept quizzing me. "Never even went visiting once?"

How could I answer that? If I said yes, she'd want to know whom he visited, and she already suspected. If I said no, I'd be lying. So I just didn't say anything. Not a word. I pretended I had a Band-Aid on my lips.

"I thought so," said Janice quietly, and left the room.

Well, I told myself, she can be upset with me if she wants, but I'm not angry at her. Actually, I knew it wasn't me she was upset with, anyway, but Dad. Yet she couldn't tell him because he didn't suspect how she felt, and even if he did, he was her boss. So I could still say I had gone through my first week of seventh grade friends with everybody, the whole world.

I really liked the idea—getting through the year without a single enemy, everybody liking Alice McKinley. It would feel good not to have one person against me, like Pamela was for a while back in sixth grade when she had the leading role in the class play, I had to be the bramble bush, and I pulled her hair on stage. Or the way Elizabeth was mad at all of us for a while last summer when her boyfriend broke up with her and she felt left out. From now on I was going to try very, very hard to get along with absolutely everybody.

I had no idea, however, what was ahead.

3 ❀ Sleeping Over

THE FOLLOWING weekend, all three of us—Pamela Jones, Elizabeth Price, and I—were a little amazed we'd survived the first two weeks of junior high. After making the mistake the first day of asking a ninth grader where the girls' gym was and being sent to the faculty lounge, finding out that the signs had been reversed on the boys' and girls' rest rooms up on second, and even after my falling down the stairs and sitting on a doughnut, we were still alive to talk about it.

"Let's have a sleepover," Elizabeth said on the bus going home. And then, as soon as we nodded our heads, she added, "We had it at my house last time."

"We had it at mine the time before," Pamela reminded us.

There was only one possible response to that: "We can have it at mine," I told them.

"For dinner or after?" Pamela asked.

"Dinner, of course," I said.

The truth is that in the year since Dad and Lester and I had moved to Silver Spring, I'd never had my friends in for an overnight except for that one week at the ocean, but that was someone else's house. I knew that the girls wanted to sleep in *my* room, in *my* house, but our house isn't exactly the overnight kind.

When we sleep over at Elizabeth's, we sleep in her bedroom with the twin beds, which we push together to sleep on crosswise, and her mother brings in platters of cookies and fruit slices with toothpicks in them. When we sleep over at Pamela's, we sleep on a hide-a-bed and a cot in the family room, and her mother makes us waffles for breakfast. At *my* house, there's a single bed in my room, and Dad's idea of a party is to buy me a bag of potato chips. Breakfast is Special K, Corn Chex, and Cheerios.

"Dad," I said as soon as he walked in the door that evening. "In forty-five minutes Pamela and Elizabeth are coming here to sleep over, and we're supposed to give them dinner."

"You're just now telling me this?"

"Well, we sort of decided it on the bus coming home—Elizabeth and Pamela did, anyway. I've *never* had them here, Dad, and I've been to their houses lots."

"True," Dad said.

"Where are they going to sleep?"

"Tell them to bring sleeping bags."

"Elizabeth doesn't have one."

"She can use Lester's, or we can get out the army
'cot in the basement," Dad said.

I swallowed. "What will we serve for dinner? It's
supposed to be something special."

Dad opened the cupboard. "Beans and franks,
Campbell's noodle, Spaghetti-O's, sardines ..."

I leaned against the wall and closed my eyes.

"Chinese ..."

"What?" My eyes popped open.

Dad was grinning. "We'll order Chinese."

I threw my arms around him.

By the time Elizabeth and Pamela came over, Lester
was on his way to pick up some cashew chicken, sweet
and sour shrimp, beef with snow peas, and fried wonton. Well, I thought to myself, maybe we don't have
the right furniture, but at least we've got the right food.

To tell the truth, our house is weird. Dad told me
once that when Mama was alive, we had regular furniture like everyone else. But then, when it was just
Dad and Lester and me, and the Melody Inn music
chain transferred Dad to Maryland, he decided that
Mom's furniture was too much to handle. So he kept
just a few pieces, gave the rest to Aunt Sally, and we
moved from Chicago to Takoma Park to Silver Spring
like gypsies, buying a few things here and there from
secondhand shops and the Door Store.

From the outside we're not too weird—just a regular
sort of two-story house, with a front porch. We live in

an old neighborhood in Silver Spring, just outside of Washington, D.C., and none of the houses are modern, so ours looks like all the rest.

But when you walk inside you don't see any rugs. You see this couch that looks like it was built out of packing crates, because it was, with cushions piled on top, and a beanbag chair, a couple of aluminum lawn chairs, and this huge round coffee table we got from Goodwill that takes up half the living room. There are brick-and-board bookcases, Dad's piano, and wherever there's a bare place on the walls, there's a poster of either some wonderful place to visit, like Barcelona or Copenhagen, or a poster about a composer. Except that some of the posters advertising places have people on them, and some of the people posters have the composer's birthplace instead. I was nine years old before I discovered that Leipzig wasn't a composer and Liszt wasn't a town in Austria.

Our kitchen is big, but the table's so small that only Dad, Lester, and I can fit around it, and our dining room is really Dad's office. The only way we can serve dinner in there is to push all his stuff over to one side of the long fold-up table. On this night, though, there wasn't time to move Dad's stuff, so when Lester came back from the China Palace with the food, we all sat on pillows on the floor around the giant coffee table and ate with chopsticks.

I could tell that this was a big deal for Pamela and Elizabeth, especially because we were eating entirely with *men*. Pamela giggled every time her knee touched

Lester's, and Elizabeth giggled whenever she dropped something with her chopsticks. We sure did a lot of giggling. I never noticed it at school, but here in the living room with Dad and Lester, it sounded really weird.

Lester, though, was the perfect gentleman. "More chicken, madam?" he asked Elizabeth.

"Another wonton, ladies?"

"Anyone for some more hot tea?"

Dad gave us a little lesson on the difference between Cantonese and Mandarin cooking, and how oyster beef doesn't have any oysters in it.

I think it would have been a normal dinner and a normal sleepover if we just hadn't read our fortune cookies. Dad's said something about the importance of being thrifty, and Dad says he hates to be preached at by a fortune cookie.

Mine was about wisdom, and Lester's was "A singing bird makes a merry heart." It was Elizabeth's and Pamela's fortunes that started the trouble.

Elizabeth takes things too seriously, anyway, and when she read hers aloud, her face turned as red as tomato soup: "A good friend will become a dear one," she said in almost a whisper.

Now if that had been anyone but Elizabeth, she would have named a few kids from school, considered the possibilities, and thrown the fortune away. Instead, she glanced sideways at Lester and blushed some more. As though Lester didn't have enough woman problems as it was. I tried to rescue him by handing

Pamela a cookie next. But when she read *her* fortune aloud, I wished I hadn't: "One touch is worth a hundred words," it said.

The problem was that her knee happened to be touching Lester's at that very moment, all of us sitting cross-legged around the coffee table. She and Elizabeth exchanged glances and then they both dissolved into giggles again. Lester didn't even catch on.

"See?" he said. "That's not a fortune, that's a proverb. I want a fortune that says, 'You will inherit a million dollars' or even 'Horrible things will happen on Wednesday.' "

Pamela and Elizabeth were still erupting in embarrassed giggles, and Dad and Lester didn't quite know what to do, so they started carrying dishes out to the kitchen and I herded the girls upstairs.

Elizabeth took the bed, Pamela got the cot, and I got Lester's smelly sleeping bag on the floor. We had Lester's portable TV for the evening, so we watched for a while, then looked through the *Seventeen* magazine that Elizabeth had brought over, but it wasn't long before I discovered that there was only one thing Pamela and Elizabeth wanted to talk about: Lester.

"He's really cute, Alice," Pamela said.

"Lester?" I said, disbelieving.

"I love his mustache," said Elizabeth dreamily. "I forget. Is his hair brown or black?"

I looked from Pamela to Elizabeth. But before I could answer, they heard Lester coming upstairs. Pamela ran to the door to peek out, then shut it in a hurry, raced back to the cot, and had another giggling fit. When Lester came out of his room again, Elizabeth peeked out and then banged the door hard and collapsed on the bed in embarrassment.

"He was going into the *bathroom!*" she said. "Oh, Alice, and he saw me looking."

"That's okay," I said. "He knows you know that he goes to the bathroom."

"I could just die," said Elizabeth.

I wondered if this is what happens to girls when they're twelve—they go bonkers over "older men." It was only a few weeks ago that Elizabeth was going to become a nun and Pamela had broken up with Mark Stedmeister, and here they were, losing their minds over Lester. *Lester!* I decided that if they didn't calm down I was going to dig up his socks from the hamper and give one to each of them, to shock them back to their senses.

"Does he have a girlfriend?" Pamela asked, as the sound of Lester's electric razor came from the bathroom.

"Yes," I told them. "Two of them. And he's probably going to marry one."

Their faces dropped. "Is he engaged?" asked Elizabeth.

"Well ... not yet," I said, and they were off again, like two horses at the starting gate. They made me turn out the light, and then they opened the door a crack and stood there watching as Lester came out of the bathroom buttoning his shirt and went into his room to put on some aftershave.

"Ohhh!" Elizabeth said weakly. "He smells *won*der-ful!"

They wanted to follow his every move, and even after he went downstairs on his way over to Marilyn's, they stood at the top of the stairs and watched him put on his jacket, then raced to a window to watch him drive away.

After they went home the next morning, I went to the Melody Inn to put in my three hours. This time Janice Sherman seemed to have undergone a personality change. She must have decided that she wasn't going to get anywhere being quiet and sad, so she was sparkly and funny instead, sort of like soda water.

"Well, Alice!" she said brightly. *Too* brightly. "What are we going to do today? Hula with Haydn? Boogie with Beethoven? A little soft shoe with Shostakovich?"

I stared. I had never heard Janice Sherman say the word *boogie* in my life. I couldn't even imagine her dancing. She was wearing a pink-and-gray plaid skirt with a pink sweater instead of her usual suit and blouse.

"Sometimes," Janice went on dreamily, "I just feel like closing up shop and flying away on a magic carpet to some far-off exotic land. Do you ever feel that way—that you'd like to do something wild and daring?"

If Crystal Harkins or Marilyn had said that, I would

have got right into the spirit of things. I'd have thought of something wild and fun I'd like to do and told them about it. But listening to Janice Sherman say it, I felt a little sad, because I knew she only wanted me to go back and tell Dad what a fun, exciting person she really was. The most daring thing I'd ever seen Janice do in the few years I'd known her was climb a stepladder.

That evening, when Dad and I were eating the left-over cashew chicken, I was about to tell him how Elizabeth and Pamela were in love with Lester when Dad said, "Al, do you remember Helen Lake?"

The name seemed familiar, but I couldn't place it. I shook my head.

"The woman who owns the beach cottage next to Janice's?"

"Oh, her," I said. "Yeah?"

"She's coming to Washington on a visit, and I've invited her and Janice Sherman to a concert."

"You've already *asked* them?" I said.

"Yes. I wrote Helen a few days ago and mentioned it to Janice this afternoon."

I stared at Dad like he had just turned into a giant toadstool. It was as though Lester had said he was going to marry both Marilyn and Crystal.

"I've been wondering if I should have the women here for dinner first—maybe Chinese, like we had last night—or take them both to a restaurant. What do you think, Al?"

"I think you have lost your mind," I said.

Dad looked up from his plate. "You don't think I

should bring them here? We'd use the dining room, of course."

"I don't think you should take them anywhere, Dad. Not together."

Dad paused with his fork in the air. "Why not?"

I couldn't believe he was so dense. "Janice Sherman will kill you! Or strangle Helen Lake, one or the other."

This time Dad put his fork down. *"Why?"*

I stared right into his eyes. "This may come as a surprise to you, Dad, but Janice has been nuts about you ever since you became manager of the Melody Inn."

For about ten seconds all you could hear in the kitchen was the hum of the refrigerator.

"You're kidding," said Dad.

I think that men and boys lack a certain chromosome or something. I mean, things happen right under their noses and they can't even see it.

"I'm not kidding. Janice has been making eyes at you for a whole year. Why do you think she let us use her beach house without charging us anything?"

"Because I'm her boss, Al, that's all. She's just trying to stay on good terms with me. That's all it is."

"Dad, Janice has been depressed ever since we got back from the ocean. She let us use her cottage for a whole week, and what did she get out of it?"

"I brought her that bushel of fresh vegetables we picked up on the way home."

"She doesn't want vegetables. She wants you! Ever since she found out you'd been visiting Helen Lake at her cottage, she's been really upset. She keeps quizzing me about what you did and who you saw while we were at Ocean City. I'm not telling you to date Janice Sherman. All I'm saying is that if you want to live a long healthy life, don't take them both out at the same time."

Dad stopped eating entirely. Every time he raised his fork to his mouth, his eyes would glaze over and he'd put it back down again. "By Jove," he said finally. And then, "Al, I wonder if you're right."

"Of course I'm right. If you proposed to Janice Sherman tomorrow, you'd be married by Tuesday."

"But what did I ever do? What did I ever say that gave her the slightest encouragement?"

"I don't know what you've said, Dad, but you've taken her to concerts now and then."

"Only as a friend. Only because we're both interested in the same music."

"*I* know that, Dad, and *you* know that, but she doesn't. I think she hoped it would lead to more."

Dad pushed his chair away from the table. "Oh, blast it!"

But the evening wasn't over yet. About six-thirty Lester came home from Maytag, and as soon as he stepped in the kitchen, he handed me a sheet of notebook paper. "Okay, Al, which one did it?"

"What?"

"Pamela or Elizabeth?" he asked.

I stared at the sheet of paper. "Lester, you are one terrific hunk," it read in big block letters. "I adore you."

My stomach sank. "Where was it?" I asked weakly.

"Under my bedroom door this morning."

Somebody, obviously, had either printed it in the night while I was asleep and slipped it under Lester's door, or done it before breakfast while the others were getting dressed. I read it again. If it had been written in script, I could have guessed, but this had me stumped.

"Pamela," I said finally. "It's got to be Pamela."

"Is she the one with the Lady Godiva hair who tried to crawl in bed with me at the beach cottage?"

"She just did it as a joke, Lester. She crawled right out again."

"Well, I don't want little notes appearing under my door, okay? I've got Marilyn and Crystal to worry about without some skinny-legged twelve-year-old spying on me and leaving notes that somebody else might see. Which one was spying on me from your room last night?"

"Both of them," I told him. "You now have four girls who would die for you, Lester. I can't understand it, but you do."

Dad understood it. "You want to go to Mexico, Les? Just the two of us?"

Lester didn't know he was kidding. "*Mexico?* When?"

"Now. Tonight. Tomorrow. I don't care."

Lester looked at Dad, then at me.

"He has *two* women who would die for him," I explained.

"Oh," said Lester.

At the bus stop on Monday, I said, "Your 'hunk' didn't think it was funny, Pamela."

"What?" said Pamela.

"That note under Lester's door. He wants you to stop spying on him and slipping notes under his door. You'll just make him mad."

"What are you *talking* about?" asked Pamela.

And then I noticed that Elizabeth's face was tomato-soup red again. I stared.

"You?" I said. And when she didn't answer, I said, "Elizabeth, I never heard you use the word *hunk* in your life."

"I figured that's what his girlfriends call him."

I still couldn't believe it. Elizabeth, the nun-to-be, having a crush on Lester the Crude.

"Elizabeth," I said earnestly, "he actually drinks catsup right out of the bottle. He sweats. He belches. He does everything you hate. There isn't anyone in the world more unlike you than Lester."

But even as I said it, I realized that Lester, in Elizabeth's eyes, would never grab a bra out of her hands and go racing around the playground with it the way Mark Stedmeister had done last summer. He would never give her an ID bracelet one week and then come back a couple weeks later to say he wanted to give it to someone else. To Pamela and Elizabeth, Lester was so far above the boys we'd been going with over the summer that he could do no wrong. I decided that the next time Lester was lifting weights and the whole basement smelled like armpits, I'd invite the girls over to see what they were missing.

In the meantime, I began to think that the main problem with love was the number three: Lester, Marilyn, and Crystal; Dad, Janice Sherman, and Helen Lake; Lester, Pamela, and Elizabeth. . . .

I was glad I wasn't part of a triangle. I was glad I didn't have a crush on anyone. For nine actual minutes that morning, I was glad to be who I was: Alice McKinley. Until I got to school.

4 ❀ Saving Dad

DAD SAYS that all my sneezing and blowing is hay fever that I probably inherited from his mother—that sometimes things like that skip a generation. Maybe so, but I don't know why this one had to skip over Dad and land on me instead of Lester, or how it could be hay fever when there isn't a barn anywhere near our neighborhood.

Just standing on the corner waiting for the bus with Pamela and Elizabeth that morning seemed to set it off, and when Patrick got on and passed my seat, he stopped and said, "What's wrong?"

"Hay fever," I told him, blowing my nose.

"Oh," said Patrick, and went on.

"See?" said Elizabeth.

"See whad?" I asked, my head stuffy.

"If Patrick was twenty instead of twelve, he would have at least sympathized or something. He wouldn't just say, 'Oh.'"

"The twenty-year-old in *my* house would have," I told her. She and Pamela were really getting dopey about older men.

In Language Arts class, first period, I sat in the row at the back, and was glad because one pocket in my jeans kept getting slimmer as I took Kleenex out, and the other pocket kept getting fatter as I stuck the used tissues back in. I knew I was really irritating Denise, the girl who sat in front of me, because every time I blew my nose, she raised her shoulders and let out a low sigh.

Over the weekend we were to have made a family tree and to have listed the most important events in our lives up to that point.

"We'll be using these charts all semester, class," Miss Summers told us. "You may want to use one of your relatives as the main character in your own original folk tale; you may want to choose an event in your own life as material for a short story; and we will be using these charts as outlines when we study autobiography and biography later on."

I wasn't listening as much as I was noticing how Miss Summers's blue-green eyes matched the color of her blouse. Then I realized she had asked us to hand our papers in, and I had just started to pass mine to Denise when I remembered we were to circle the name of anyone who was dead or absent.

"Wait a minute," I said, as my nose started running again, and, snatching my paper back, I circled the penciled box that said, "Mother," holding a Kleenex over my nose, while Denise watched impatiently.

"Oooh!" she said, taking my paper again. "Widdle Alwice don't have her a mama." And laughed.

I didn't think much of it, because people say stupid things all the time. I took still another Kleenex and blew hard. When I got to Phys. Ed., though, I remembered something else I hadn't done. We were supposed to have freshly laundered shorts and T-shirts, and I'd forgotten to take mine home. In the lineup, the teacher told me that having clean clothes at inspection every two weeks would be part of my grade, and then I heard the large girl somewhere down the line say, "But Widdle Alwice don't have a mommy!" and some of the other girls giggled.

"Do you know anything about that girl over there?" I asked Elizabeth at lunch.

"Denise Whitlock?" Elizabeth said. "She's an eighth grader, but I heard she's repeating a couple courses this year."

I noticed that Denise always sat with the same three girls in the cafeteria, all older than we, and they always seemed to be looking around, whispering about other people, and laughing. I decided to steer clear of Denise.

But in World Studies that afternoon, as we went in the door, Patrick said, "I heard you were crying in Language Arts this morning."

I stared at him. "I *wasn't!*"

He just shrugged. "Somebody said you were crying because your mother's dead."

"That's *dumb*, Patrick! I was blowing my nose because I have hay fever."

"Oh," said Patrick, and this time *I* wished he could think of a little more to say.

I took my seat in the first desk in the front row. World Studies is one of the subjects where I get butterflies in the stomach, because I always know I'll be called on first.

Mr. Hensley was talking about Russia and its republics and was pacing back and forth in front of the room. Not only did he have bad breath, I had discovered, but he spewed little droplets of saliva on the people in the first row. I was thinking how funny it would be if I came to school some day with an umbrella and held it over my head—how the other kids would laugh—when suddenly I saw Mr. Hensley stop in front of me.

"Alice, can you tell us in what ways Russia, before 1861, was similar to the United States before the Civil War?"

It's questions that come at me like Ping-Pong balls that unnerve me. My mind goes blank. I could feel my face turning red.

"Um ... there were sections of the country that didn't agree with other sections of the country?" I said at last. I'm not stupid, but I'm not the brightest person in seventh grade, either.

Mr. Hensley smiled patiently. "Well, yes, but that's still the case, isn't it? There are over 150 national groups living in Russia, remember, each with its own language and customs. But why is the year 1861 important? Yes, Patrick?"

"Alexander II proclaimed freedom for the serfs," said Patrick. "Before that they could be bought and sold, just like here."

"Correct. Alexander II began his reign as a reformer. What else was he responsible for?" Mr. Hensley asked. Patrick named all the accomplishments like the letters of the alphabet. I didn't relax until the bell rang and I knew I wouldn't be called on again.

At home, we try not to save up all our gripes and bring them up at the dinner table. "When I get home from work," Dad always says, "I don't feel like eating problems." But sometimes we find ourselves laying them out on the table, anyway.

Lester started it by coming to dinner in a rotten mood and complaining because we were eating canned macaroni. Dad remarked that he was in a foul mood himself and wasn't up to anyone else's complaining, and Lester said that whatever Dad's problem was, it couldn't be worse than his own.

"Want to bet?" Dad said. "I've invited both Janice Sherman and Helen Lake to a concert this Saturday, but if what Alice tells me is true and Janice Sherman really does think she's in love with me, it's a crazy idea."

"It's a crazy idea," said Lester, biting into his garlic bread like he was attacking it. "Take it from me, Dad, it's a ridiculous idea. Marilyn told me last night I've got to choose between her and Crystal, and it's driving me nuts."

"Hmmm," said Dad in sympathy.

We ate in silence for a while, except for the occasional crunch of garlic bread.

"Well," I said, trying to divert their attention. "In Language Arts, a girl teased me because Mom's dead."

Dad looked up. "People don't tease about things like that, Al."

"Yeah?" I said. "She did it again in gym." I explained what happened, and added, "Now it's going around school that I was crying in class because I don't have a mother."

"Anyone who would tease about that is just plain sick," said Dad. "Ignore it."

"How?" I asked. "I've never been good at pretending I'm deaf."

"The next time she says something to you about Mom, just look at her and say, 'Yeah? And your mother wears army boots,' " said Lester.

Sometimes Dad and Lester are *worse* than no help to me whatsoever.

"Of course," Lester added, "Dad could always marry Janice or Helen, and then you'd have a mother, and that would shut her up."

"Shut up, Lester," said Dad.

As the evening went on, though, and after I'd found some cheesecake at the back of the refrigerator that Lester had probably hidden from me, I began to feel a lot better. I began to feel, in fact, that Dad's and

Lester's problems were a hundred times worse than mine. Lester would simply have to solve his himself, but Dad was in a real mess. Unlike Lester, he already knew for sure which woman he liked best, and it wasn't the one he had to work with every day, which really made things sticky. I decided to call Aunt Sally in Chicago and see what she had to suggest.

"Alice," she said. "It's so good to hear from you. How's seventh grade?"

I'd already decided I wasn't going to tell her any of my problems, not when I was being charged by the minute, so I said that things were going great with me, but I was worried about Dad.

There was silence at the other end of the line—the kind of silence when you can still hear someone breathing.

"What's he done, Alice?" she said.

"*Nothing!* It's just that there are these two women ..."

"*What* women?"

"Well, the assistant manager of his store, and then the one he met at the beach."

"I *knew* it!" said Aunt Sally.

"What?"

"I knew he'd go crazy with grief after your mother died. All these years he's been so quiet...."

"He's really okay, Aunt Sally. It's just that he likes this one woman a lot, the one he met at the beach, but he's invited them both to a concert, and—"

"Why on earth would he do something like that?"

The thing about Aunt Sally is that to get her to listen, you have to shut her up. I finally explained how he'd always thought of Janice Sherman as his business partner, while she always thought of him as . . . well, something more. I could just tell.

"And this girl he met on the beach?"

"*At* the beach," I corrected. "She's not a girl, Aunt Sally, she's a lady. She owned the beach cottage next to ours."

"Well, I'm *so* glad you called," said my aunt. "This is the kind of thing that could get your father in serious trouble."

"How?"

"If things go along the way they are, with that Sherman woman thinking he might marry her, he could get hit with a breach of promise suit."

I had no idea it was so serious. I had no idea, either, what a breach of promise suit even was. But the way Aunt Sally made it sound, it was like bubonic plague or something.

"What's Janice Sherman like?" Aunt Sally asked.

I tried to describe Janice. I said she wasn't too short, not too tall, not too fat, not too thin, she was pretty but not exactly beautiful, and she loved music.

"Aha!" Aunt Sally seemed to be thinking. "Well, I don't know if Ben wants any suggestions from me, Alice, but I've got one."

"We'll try anything," I said. Not checking with Dad, of course.

"It worked for a neighbor of mine. His wife died a

while back, and some woman was always chasing him every chance she got. If she wasn't bringing him meatloaf, she was bringing him applesauce. So one day he told her that while he found her very attractive, it wouldn't be fair to get involved with her because she reminded him so much of his wife."

I tried to figure that one out.

"He said if they were to get serious about each other, he'd expect her to look and laugh and dress and behave just like his wife."

"What happened?"

"That's all it took. Once she knew she'd have to live up to what some other woman had been, that poor soul turned on her heels and never knocked on his door again. Not only did she stop taking him applesauce, she never asked for her bowl back."

"That's all Dad has to do?"

"He should just tell Janice that every time he looks at her, he feels sad. She'll be grateful to him for telling her, she'll be flattered that he's so fond of her, and she'll understand completely. Believe me, as a woman, I just know."

I lay on my bed a long time that evening, staring down at the rug, knowing Dad would never tell Janice that. I wondered how something as wonderful as love could make so many people unhappy, and tried to think if there wasn't some other way to handle this. Like having Lester take Janice Sherman to the concert while Dad took Helen Lake.

"Lester," I said, from the doorway of his room, "would you ever date an older woman?"

Lester looked up from the textbook he was studying. "Older than what?"

"Older than you."

"Depends," said Lester, and made some notes in his notebook.

"Just for a single evening?" I went on. "If it would save somebody's life?"

Lester put down his pen. "Al, what the heck are you talking about?"

"Dad's in a real mess with Janice and Helen. You just *know* if he takes them both to the concert it's going to be a horrible evening."

"Al, Dad's a big boy. He can take care of himself. And if you think I'm going to take Janice Sherman to the concert and have *both* Marilyn and Crystal mad at me, you're wrong. The answer is no! Nix! Nyet!"

That was pretty definite. The only thing left to do was to tell Janice Sherman myself just how much she reminded Dad of Mom.

I went to the Melody Inn the next day after school because I felt that if Janice Sherman wasn't expecting me, it might be easier to talk. Sometimes, when I rehearse things in advance, the words come out stupid sounding, so I didn't practice. I decided I'd just say what came naturally and see what happened. What happened was that Janice said, "Alice, what are you doing here on a Tuesday?" and I said, "I want to talk to you about my dad." I mean, how natural can you get?

Dad was at the front of the store showing a grand piano to a woman who looked as though she could afford fifty of them, so Janice knew we'd be alone for a while.

"Sit down, Alice," she said gently, shutting the door to the office. "What is it? What about your father?"

I swallowed and sat down. The words seemed stuck inside me, though. What was I supposed to say next? I took a deep breath. "It's about you and Dad," I said, and stopped again.

Janice Sherman was sitting on the edge of her chair, and I had the feeling that if I didn't say more soon, she'd fall forward right into my lap. So I said, "I think you know that Dad likes you very much."

Janice blushed and smiled in surprise. She twisted the chain around her neck. "We *do* get along well as co-workers, Alice. But ... other than that ... well, I guess your dad will just have to speak for himself. *I'm* very fond of *him*, of course."

"I know," I said, "and that's why I want to say something because ..." Uh oh, I thought as I saw her stiffen, "because ... well, the real truth is that you remind Dad a lot of my mom."

Janice Sherman stared.

"And ... Dad knows how unfair it would be to you ... I mean, to fall in love with a woman who resembled his first wife."

I could tell that Janice was confused. *I* was confused.

She had to be flattered, though, that Dad was fond of her and that she reminded him of someone he'd once chosen to marry, so she said, real softly, "Tell me about your mother, Alice. What was she like?"

I wanted to run right to the phone and tell Aunt Sally that everything she said was right. Janice Sherman *did* understand, and she'd be grateful forever. She might not get Dad, and they'd live their separate lives, but deep inside, she would know that there was this wonderful unfulfilled passion. . . .

For the first time that day, I felt my shoulders begin to relax.

"Well," I said, trying to remember everything I'd ever heard about my mother. "I was only five when she died, so I don't remember her that well, but Aunt Sally says she had a good sense of humor, she always joked a lot. I think she had sort of reddish-blond hair. She never liked oatmeal; Dad told me that. And Lester says she was sort of tall and always wore slacks, and she sang a lot. Especially songs from musicals. And freckles. She had freckles."

I was going to go on but I realized suddenly that Janice Sherman wasn't smiling anymore. Janice Sherman wasn't even sitting. She got up as stiffly as if her legs were made of wood.

"That description," she said, her chin trembling a little, "fits Helen Lake exactly, and your f-father seems to find *her* very easy to get along with indeed." And she headed for the rest room.

I felt awful. I left the office at the back of the store

and walked right by the Gift Shoppe where a revolving display case lights up when you press a button.

"We got some cute Beethoven bikinis in, Alice," Loretta Jenkins said, pushing back the clump of wild curly hair that hung around her face like a mane. She grinned at me but I shook my head.

"No? What about our new Stravinsky T-shirts?"

"I'm just not in the shopping mood today," I told her, and went home. I decided that Lester was right. Dad was a big boy and could take care of himself, and I had no business saying what I did to Janice Sherman. I hoped Dad would never find out.

What happened was that Dad got a phone call from Helen Lake two days before the concert saying she had to go into the hospital for some knee surgery, that she was *so* sorry, but she'd be coming to Washington again in November, and she'd make it up to him then. Dad was disappointed, of course, but the fact that she was coming in November gave him something to look forward to, and the thought that he didn't have to take both her and Janice out together was a tremendous relief.

The morning of the concert, though, Janice Sherman called in sick at the Melody Inn and said she had a migraine and hoped Dad would understand that she couldn't possibly attend the concert.

"You want to go to the Kennedy Center tonight and hear the National Symphony?" Dad asked me at dinner.

"Sure, Dad," I said, wanting to give him every little bit of comfort that I could.

"Les, you want to go?" Dad said. "I've got three tickets."

"What are they playing?" asked Lester, his mouth full of potato.

"Schubert, Vivaldi, and Brahms," said Dad.

"Spare me," said Lester.

So Dad and I went to the concert alone, he bought me a three-dollar Coke at intermission, and I put my jacket on the empty seat.

5 ❀ Celebrity

IT WAS the fourth week of school when I thought of the seventh good thing about junior high, to cancel out the seven bad things. But before the week was over, I discovered an eighth bad thing that sounded so awful, so terrible, that it canceled out all seven of the good.

I woke up one morning remembering that while we had General Music, we didn't have to sing unless we wanted to. We could play a tune on a recorder instead. No more lining up to walk to the all-purpose room, where a woman at the piano taught you a song. No more teachers making us sing it row by row, then two by two, until they found out where that awful sound was coming from—namely, me. I would never have to sing another note in front of people in my life unless I wanted. Which I didn't.

Patrick thinks it's weird that I'm the only one in my family who can't carry a tune. Lester says that Mom sang all the time; Dad sings and plays the piano, the flute, and the violin; Lester can play a trumpet, sing, and play a guitar. I don't do anything but sort of hum to myself when I'm running the vacuum cleaner.

Last summer Patrick taught me to play some duets with him on our piano, and I did fine. It's just that when I try to hum a tune, what comes out of my mouth doesn't sound like music at all—to Patrick, to anyone. The worst part is that I can't tell the difference.

"So have me tested! Operate!" I told Dad the last time he brought it up, and he said he'd never mention it again. He didn't.

Pamela and Elizabeth, of course, promptly joined the Seventh Grade Chorus, and Patrick joined the band. He became second drummer, and on the days he had practice, his dad drove him to school with his drums and cymbals in the back seat.

I didn't join anything. I wasn't sure I wanted to join something the first year of junior high. Maybe I just wanted to watch what the other kids did and make up my mind later.

"You're not going out for *any*thing, Alice?" Pamela asked. "You really should, you know."

"Why?"

"To meet people."

"I'm meeting people all the time! I'm meeting people every time I walk in a classroom!"

"But you don't really get a chance to *do* anything with them or *go* anywhere," Pamela continued. "My cousin in New Jersey says that you should join everything you possibly can, because even if it's only a girls' club, most girls have brothers, and the brothers have friends, and it's sort of like taking out an insurance policy that by the time the ninth-grade formal comes along, someone will fix you up."

"Fix me up?"

"You know, make sure you have a date—that someone invites you."

"I'd rather someone invited me all by himself."

"Oh, Alice, you just don't understand how things work," Pamela sighed.

That night Lester and I were making tostados for dinner—I was chopping the cheese and lettuce, and Lester was cooking the beef and beans.

"Les," I said, "did anyone ever fix you up on a date?"

"A few times," he told me. "Disasters, mostly."

"What happened?"

"Nothing. That's the trouble."

I gave him my disapproving "Aunt Sally" look, but that wasn't what Lester meant.

"No sparks," he said. "No music. Just one big missmatch."

I took the tostado shells out of the microwave and helped Lester pile on the stuff. "I'm not ever going to let anyone fix me up with anybody."

"Oh, I wouldn't go *that* far, Al. That's how I met Crystal, after all."

"You *did*?"

Les nodded. "I was really hurting after Marilyn broke up with me, and one of the guys knew this girl who had a sister who had a friend ... that kind of thing. It was Crystal."

Lester and I sat down across the table from each other, putting some food aside for Dad because he was working late.

"What's going to happen with you and Crystal and Marilyn?" I asked him.

I thought he might tell me it was none of my business, but he didn't.

"It's up to Marilyn now," he said. "I told her if she's ready to get engaged, I'll give her a ring and give up Crystal. If she's not ... well, I don't want to be jilted again."

I picked up all the little pieces of cheese on my plate, mashed them with my finger, and put them in my mouth all at once. "What did she say, Les?"

"She's thinking about it. The ball's in her court, now."

"I like them both," I said. "A *lot*."

"Yeah, that's the trouble. So do I."

The next day at school, something absolutely *wonderful* happened. The cafeteria was serving hamburgers on poppyseed rolls, the only food they make that's any good, and Pamela and Elizabeth and I had just eaten ours and were heading outside, sharing a bag of Fritos, when we saw two ninth-grade boys standing in the doorway. I noticed that one of them was holding a notebook and pen, and the other had a camera. Just as we reached the door, the one with the pen said, "Hi. You a seventh grader?"

I waited for Pamela or Elizabeth to answer, then realized he was looking right at me. I nodded.

"Well, I'm the roving reporter for the *Eagle* and this is our photographer. I wondered if we could interview you for the school paper."

I stared. *"Me?"*

"If you don't mind," he said. "We choose a different person every issue—help students get acquainted."

Not Pamela with her long blond hair? Not Elizabeth with her creamy complexion and thick black eyelashes? Me, Alice McKinley, with this sort of blondish-reddish hair and freckles?

"Uh ... I guess so," I said. We went out in the hall, where Pamela and Elizabeth sat down on a register to wait.

I sat down on a bench facing the reporter while the photographer tinkered with his camera.

"Okay now," the reporter said. "You're ..."

"Alice McKinley," I said, and spelled it for him.

"What are your favorite subjects?"

"Uh ... Language Arts and Life Science. I guess."

"Worst subject?"

"World Studies." Oh, boy, wouldn't I be popular with Hensley when he read that?

"Joined any clubs yet?"

"Not yet."

"What do you think of junior high so far?"

The interview lasted about five minutes. Every time I gave an answer, I realized how stupid it would look in the paper and wished I'd said something else. The boy with the camera took three different pictures of me and said he'd print the best one. Then the interview was over and they left. Pamela and Elizabeth rushed over.

"Alice!" Pamela squealed. "You're going to be in the newspaper!"

"What did they ask?" Elizabeth cried.

"What did you say?" both of them asked together.

I could feel my face blushing, and told them everything I could remember.

"Why do you suppose they chose you?" asked Pamela finally.

I guess that wasn't exactly a compliment. I would have liked to think it was my beautiful smile or my glowing hair or my gorgeous figure or something. But I was so excited and surprised I didn't worry too much about it. I was going to be in the *paper*!

There was a pep assembly that afternoon. Everybody had to go, but I didn't mind. I practically floated to the top row of the bleachers, anyway, I felt so high. The band was playing the school song, and I could see Patrick playing the cymbals.

What a pep assembly is, see, is where they introduce the members of the basketball team, and everybody cheers, and then they tell you how important it is for everybody to go to the next game. The cheerleaders come out on the floor to teach you a few yells, the band plays the school song again, and then everybody sings it. Everybody but me, of course. I just mouthed the words and nobody cared. I was going to appear in the newspaper, and I couldn't even sing, and nobody cared! It was wonderful.

When the assembly was over, though, and we were all crowding out the door, I was busy talking to Elizabeth and accidentally bumped into the girl on the other side of me. It was Denise. Denise Whitlock.

"Sorry," I said.

She frowned and rubbed her arm where my notebook had scraped.

"Sorry," I said again.

Denise smiled then, but it wasn't a real smile; sort of a "poor you" kind of look. She waited until I had moved slightly ahead of her, and then she said, "SGSD."

"What?" I said, turning, not knowing if she was swearing or talking to me.

She just laughed, and the other three girls with her laughed, too.

"What did she mean, 'SGSD'?" I asked Pamela.

"I don't know. She's weird. Forget her," said Pamela.

I think I would have forgotten about it if I hadn't seen those same initials scribbled on the blackboard in math class, down in one corner, and Denise isn't even in that class. It was when I saw it scribbled on a locker, though, and then on the sidewalk in front of the flagpole, that I got a little worried.

"What do you suppose it means?" I asked some of

my other friends, but no one seemed to know, not even Patrick.

In the cafeteria the next day, Denise and her girl-friends were laughing, looking around and whispering the way they do, and suddenly they started chanting, "S–G–S–D, S–G–S–D," and they laughed again. People turned and looked at them and went on eating, but a few chanted it along with them. It gave me the creeps.

And then, after school, Elizabeth had the answer. She told us on the bus going home. Her eyes were huge as we squeezed in beside her on the very back seat.

"I asked a girl in P.E., an eighth grader," she said breathlessly, "and she told me that every fall, the upper classmen pick one certain day and call it 'Seventh Grade Sing Day'—SGSD—and on that day, they can stop any seventh grader in the halls and ask him to sing the school song. If he can't, he gets dunked in the water fountain, if he's lucky; in the toilets, if he's not."

I felt as though someone had just told me I'd be executed.

"When?" I asked. "I'll stay home! I'll be sick!"

"People don't find out until they get to school," Elizabeth said, chewing her lip. "They never tell you in advance."

"The teachers just let them *do* it?" I choked.

"It's against the rules, this girl said, but the faculty isn't too strict about it. Sometimes the principal gets on the loud speaker and says there will be no dunking, but there is, anyway. Teachers can't be everywhere at once."

I stared at Pamela, then Elizabeth. "What are we going to do?" I bleated.

"Learn the school song!" said Elizabeth. "Sometimes they let you off with just one verse, but sometimes they ask you to sing all three. And they always make you sing it at the top of your lungs, with everyone looking. I guess it's like an initiation."

I knew then what it was like to live on Death Row. There were rumors that SGSD would be the following Tuesday, or Wednesday, or Thursday, but the days came and went and it never happened. I began to think that maybe this year they were going to let it slide.

On Friday, the school newspaper came out, the issue with my picture in it. The teacher passed the papers out in homeroom, and kids kept turning around saying, "Alice! You're in the paper! You're a celebrity!"

I opened mine to page three. The column was about five inches long, and the photograph was okay. I mean, I was smiling really big, but it wasn't a fake smile; I didn't look as though I were sitting on ice cubes or anything. I wished that the lock of hair down over my eyes had been tucked behind one ear instead, but it wasn't so bad.

It was a weekly feature called, "Getting to Know . . ." and this time it said, "Getting to Know Alice McKinley."

Meet Alice, a seventh grader, who likes Language Arts and Life Science, but says that World Studies is only so-so. What this photo doesn't show is that Alice has blondish hair, freckles, and stands about five-foot-two in her stocking feet, except that she was wearing Reeboks.

'Al,' as her family calls her, lives with her father and brother, and moved here a year ago from Takoma Park. Chicago, before that. What she misses about Chicago is the lake. What she loves about Maryland is that we're close to the ocean. So she's not hard to please.

Her favorite food is french-fried onions. Her favorite music is country rock. She hasn't decided yet on a career—maybe a veterinarian, she says, or a basketball player. (You'll have to grow a little, Alice, to do that!)

So far she hasn't joined any clubs; she just wants to look around and take her time. We think it won't be long before she finds a lot to do here. We hope so, anyway. Welcome, Miss McKinley!

I couldn't believe that I came out sounding halfway intelligent and that the photo was okay. I couldn't help grinning. The girls in back of me couldn't believe it, either.

"I think they purposely choose an unknown," one of them said. "You know, if they chose people everybody knew, there wouldn't be any point in writing about them."

I didn't care. Nothing could hurt me now. Even when I saw Elizabeth in the hall, and she said, "It's a wonderful write-up, Alice, except for the photo."

"What's wrong with it?"

"Didn't you *see*?" asked Elizabeth.

"See what?"

Elizabeth unfolded her copy of the paper and pointed. "That poppyseed there between your teeth. It shows."

It wasn't more than a dot—a speck. It could have been merely a flaw in the paper. It didn't bother me at all.

But as I went through the door in Language Arts, Denise Whitlock made a point of bumping *my* arm.

"Soon," she said. "SGSD."

6  SGSD

I FINALLY told Dad and Lester about it. I guess I hadn't wanted them to know that there was anything in junior high I couldn't handle myself, but the middle of the next week at breakfast, when I ate only half a piece of toast for the third day in a row because my stomach hurt, Dad looked at me and said simply, "Al, what's wrong?"

There's a certain way a father says that that makes your chin tremble and the corners of your mouth turn down, and I sat there trying not to bawl. Finally, though, I blurted it all out—about Denise and her gang, and the possibility that I would either get dunked in the toilets or have to sing to a crowd of fifty at the top of my lungs.

"Well, Al," Lester said from across the table where

he was eating a slice of leftover pizza along with his Corn Chex, "it could be worse. You could sing to a crowd of fifty at the top of your lungs and get dunked in the toilet *because* of it."

"That doesn't help, Les," Dad said, and turned to me. "All I can suggest, sweetheart, is that if it happens, carry it off with as much good humor as you can muster."

"Dad, I c-can't!" I stammered, and felt the tears. "The worse you sing the f-first verse, the more likely they'll make you sing the second and third."

"So sing the second and third and act like you're enjoying yourself," Dad told me. "They'll take their cues from you. If you're embarrassed, they'll stare and whisper. But if you look like you're enjoying it, they'll lose interest."

I didn't for a moment believe it. We ate in silence, and finally Lester said, "Dad, do you remember the junior high band I played in back in Chicago?"

"Yes?"

"Remember how on Wednesdays a bus picked up band members from all the area schools and took us to a high school auditorium where we practiced together in one group?"

"Yes, I remember."

"Well, what I never told you was that every so often one of the guys lost his pants."

"What?"

"A guy would get his pants pulled off and thrown out the window of the bus. It was sort of a tradition.

We'd get to where we were going, and there would be one kid who, if he couldn't fight the older guys off, would be in his underpants for the rehearsal. The bus driver never caught on, the band director never caught on—there were too many of us. Whichever kid was chosen, his friends would sort of crowd around him to shield him from view, so the adults never found out. Or if they did, they never did anything about it."

"Why didn't someone report it?"

"That's the part I always wondered," Lester said. "But nobody did. We probably figured if we told, we'd *really* get it. I suppose it happened maybe five or six times during the whole school year, and I don't know what those five or six kids told their parents about their pants."

Dad studied Lester over his coffee. "How come you never told me?"

"I don't know. I've thought about that, too. I guess I figured there was nothing you could do—it was just something I had to deal with myself. But for a whole year, I dreaded Wednesdays. I used to lie awake half of Tuesday night worrying about it, and I quit band the next year. But I never said why."

I sat there looking at my brother, imagining him back in seventh grade worrying about losing his pants in front of all the other kids. I'd never thought Lester would be embarrassed about anything, but now I knew. Which was worse, I wondered—having to sing in front of fifty kids when you can't carry a tune, or having to go to band practice in your underpants. I wasn't sure.

"When is this Seventh Grade Sing Day going to be?" Lester asked.

"That's the worst part. Nobody knows. Soon. Monday, probably. I'm not so worried about before or after school, because there's just enough time to get from the bus to the building and back again It's the lunch period that scares me. You have to eat and then either go outside or to the library. You can't stay in the cafeteria the whole period. And I hear the eighth and ninth graders guard the library so you can't get in."

"Well, Al, the worst that can happen is that they'll embarrass you. But you'll still be alive the next day," Dad said, as though that was any comfort.

SGSD didn't happen on Monday, but the rumors went around like wildfire. Everywhere I went I heard the whispers: "Tomorrow ... tomorrow ... tomorrow ..."

I *really* had a stomachache that night. I think I ate one french fry and two bites of hamburger.

"Everybody says it will be tomorrow," I told Dad. "*Please* can't I stay home?"

"You going to run away, Al, when the going gets tough?"

"Yes."

"Going to let Denise and her gang know they can scare you off?"

"Yes."

"So they'll be even bolder when they try something else?"

I thought about that a moment. "No," I said finally, and the next day I went to school.

All three of us—Elizabeth, Pamela, and I—sat huddled together on one seat of the bus, as though somehow we could protect ourselves by sticking together. Of the three of us, Pamela was the least concerned. The same Pamela who got the lead part in our sixth-grade play because she could sing probably knew she could carry it off if anybody backed her against the wall. In fact, the way she was chattering on and on about it, I figured she sort of hoped she *would* be cornered in the hallway, because she loved an audience.

Elizabeth was scared, though. She was afraid she'd forget the words to the second and third verses and kept wanting to recite them to me to make sure she had them right. Mostly, she was afraid that if she was dunked in the drinking fountain, her hair would look awful, and if she was dunked in the toilets, she'd throw up.

I wasn't as worried about the drinking fountain or toilets as I was about the humiliation of opening my mouth and letting pure noise come out.

As soon as we were inside the school, Elizabeth, Pamela, and I stuck together as long as we could before we had to separate to go to different homerooms. I saw Patrick walking down the hall ahead of me and ran to catch up with him. I knew that if anyone came up to me when I was with Patrick and asked me to sing, Patrick would sing it for me if he could. Or sing along with me. He's like that.

"Hi," I said, wedging myself between him and the wall and getting in step.

Patrick guessed right away. "You know what day it is, huh?"

"*Is* it? Patrick, are you sure?"

"I heard someone say so on the bus. Nobody's letting on until after the morning announcements, because they don't want the principal trying to head it off."

"P-Patrick!" I gulped, in a small squeaky voice, like a chicken. "What am I going to do?"

"About what?" he said. And you know, that was one of the nicest things he ever said to me, because it meant he'd forgotten all about how I can't sing. When you think something's wrong with you, you believe that everyone is thinking about it all the time. Like it's the only important thing about you. But Patrick actually *had* forgotten.

"I can't *sing!*" I told him.

"Oh. *That,*" he said. "Well, just pretend you have laryngitis, Alice. Open your mouth, move your lips, and point to your throat."

I knew that wouldn't work with Denise and her crowd if she got hold of me. I'd have to go all day long not talking to anyone, not even teachers, and still, I'll bet, no one would believe me. "Patrick," I said, "what are you doing after lunch? I mean, you want to go out and sit on the wall with me?"

"There's going to be an extra band rehearsal," he said. "All the percussion players have to be there."

My last hope. As I ducked into homeroom, Patrick said, "Cheer up, Alice. It's not the end of your life."

Maybe not for Patrick, who could play the drums, the cymbals, the marimba, and the piano and could belt out songs like he'd written them himself. But it could be the end of my life in seventh grade as I'd known it up to then. I wondered if anyone ever died of embarrassment, if the heart just stopped beating or something.

I sat clutching my books to my chest while the homeroom teacher collected health forms, then sat some more while the principal made the daily announcements. Finally, when the bell rang, I took a deep breath and plunged into the hallway.

I hadn't even got to my first class before I saw some guy backed up against the lockers and two ninth graders, holding his arms, making him sing. The poor kid was singing in a soft little voice, and the older boys kept saying, "Louder! We can't hear you! Louder!" The boy's face was as pink as bubble gum. Other kids stopped to watch and laugh. I wished my picture had never been in the school newspaper. Now everyone knew I was a seventh grader. Somebody tried to grab my arm and stop me just before I ducked into Language Arts, but I made it. I even got there before Denise and sat with my heart pounding. When she came in, she gave me her usual "poor you" smile and said nothing.

I don't think the teachers even knew about SGSD yet. Miss Summers, who wears Obsession perfume (I know because she smells just like Crystal Harkins, and that's what Crystal wears), talked about words that had more than one meaning, such as "funny," which could mean either hilarious or peculiar, and I decided that the most peculiar thing of all was that there was torture and horror going on right under the teachers' noses and they didn't even recognize it.

By lunchtime, no one had caught me yet, but I could see Denise and her friends eyeing me from three tables away. When they left the cafeteria before I did, I knew they were up to something.

"Well, I haven't been stopped all morning!" said Pamela, and I think she actually was disappointed. "All this worry for nothing. I'm going right out on the school steps after lunch and get some sun."

"I'm going to go in a rest room and bolt the door to a toilet and sit there till the bell rings," Elizabeth said shakily.

"What about the library?" I asked.

"I already looked," Elizabeth said. "There are ninth graders stationed at both ends of the hall. They grab you before you even get to the door."

I wasn't going to sit outside with Pamela, but I wasn't going to lock myself in a toilet, either. If Denise saw me going into a rest room, she'd simply corner me in a stall. I tried to think of where I could go that kids usually didn't and finally decided on the faculty parking lot. I'd sit down between the principal and vice-principal's cars. It was the only place I could think of that I had any chance at all.

When we were through eating, I walked to the main door of the cafeteria and peered out to make sure Denise wasn't there. Then, while Elizabeth headed for a rest room and Pamela went right out the front entrance, just begging to be caught, I slipped around to a side door and headed across the grass toward the faculty lot.

I could hear someone singing the school song in front of the building. I saw a girl backed up against a tree out near the sidewalk, a group of older students gathered around her saying, "Second verse! Louder!"

And just as I started down the row of parked cars, I saw Denise and her gang coming toward me. I stopped, and it seemed as though the whole world had stopped turning.

It was sort of like standing out in the middle of the road watching a truck bear down on you. I knew that if I turned around and ran, they'd catch me. If I went left, I was up against the brick building. If I went right, I'd be out in the middle of traffic. If I continued straight ahead ...

This is what it's like to die, I told myself, and leaned against a car as Denise came toward me.

"Hey, Widdle Alwice," said Denise.

I tried smiling. I couldn't even fake it.

"Your mama teach you to sing?" Denise went on, and the three other girls giggled. One was tall and stoop-shouldered, one was short and square, and the other had a face full of zits. They were four girls who acted as though nobody could possibly like them very much, so nobody did.

"We want to hear the school song," the tall one said, squinting her eyes at me.

The short girl started yelping, "Song! Song!" to call other kids over, and people started coming from all directions, like ants at a picnic.

Denise nudged my arm. "We're waiting," she said. "Sing."

"I-I can't," I said. "I know the words, but I can't sing. I can say them for you, though."

Did you ever see the way lions and tigers sort of walk around their food before they tear into it? The purring noise they make? That's what Denise was doing right then—the way her eyes started to smile, her lips started to stretch. Soft laughter began at the back of her throat and worked its way out.

"No good," she said. "We want to hear you *sing* it, Widdle Alwice. When you go to basketball games, you have to be able to sing. How are you going to help the team along if you're just standing there saying the words?"

"Sing! Sing! Sing! Sing!" the other three girls began to chant, and then some of the other kids joined in. "Sing! Sing! Sing! Sing!"

"I can't," I said again.

The kids crowded in closer. It was probably the nearest Denise had ever come in her life to being onstage, the most attention she had ever got. "You can't *sing*?" she asked in mock horror. "What's the matter? Is your singer broken? Every American girl can sing." She nudged me a little harder. "*Try* it."

I shook my head and stared at the ground. I felt like I was going to throw up and imagined puking all over Denise's Nikes. I imagined her knocking the daylights out of me.

"Maybe she needs to spray her throat first with a little toilet water," the girl with the zits said.

"Yeah, a little dunk in the toilet might help," the tall girl suggested.

"I can't sing," I told them again. "I never could."

"Well, we want to hear what it sounds like, anyway," said Denise. She was really enjoying herself now and was talking louder so everyone could hear. "Everyone listen, now. Widdle Alwice is going to try."

They crowded in closer still. They were all grinning.

"Last chance," said Denise. "Do or dunk. Which will it be?" She turned to the short girl beside her. "You know that toilet up on second? The one that doesn't flush? Widdle Alwice is going to smell real nice after we dunk her in that one."

I knew exactly which toilet they were talking about. It always stunk, and it was filled almost to the top with toilet paper and crud.

Why couldn't the principal look out of his window right now and see what was going on? Why couldn't Patrick get out of band practice early and come rescue me? Why couldn't real life be like fairy stories once in a while where there's always a prince when you need him?

"Sing!" Denise ordered, starting to sound angry, and then, somewhere behind me, I heard my name.

"Hey, Al."

I turned. It was Lester. I couldn't believe it.

Everyone else turned, too. Lester was strolling across the driveway, and I could see his car parked out by the curb.

"Hey, Al!" he said again. "How you doin'?" He was making like we weren't related, I knew. Just a friend who had dropped by.

I didn't know what to say. But Lester took over. "I was driving by, saw you out here, and thought I'd stop," he said, putting one arm around my shoulder and walking me out of the circle. "What's up? What's been happening lately?"

Denise and her friends stared after us. I could see Denise's eyes as I walked away, small and squinty with that "I'll-get-you" look. The other kids began to wander off and finally, when Les and I got around to a tree and were by ourselves, I tried hard not to bawl.

"They almost had me, Lester," I said shakily.

"I sort of figured that," he said, and put his hands in his pockets. "How long before lunch period is over?"

I looked at my watch. "Four or five minutes."

"I'll hang around," he said. "It'll only make me a few minutes late to class." He looked over to where

Denise and her gang were still standing. "The hefty one. That's Denise?"

I sniffled and nodded. "I couldn't do it, Les. I couldn't sing. They were going to dunk me in a toilet up on second that's been stopped up for a month."

"Well, after today, SGSD is over, isn't it? Think you can get out of the building at two-thirty and onto the bus?"

"Sure."

I don't know what we talked about for the next five minutes. Lester did the talking, I guess, trying to make it look as though we were catching up on news. He walked me around to the door that was just outside my math class, and when the bell rang, I said, "Thanks, Les," went inside, and Lester left.

It was nice to know he'd been concerned about me—that he actually cared enough to drive over and see what was happening before he went to the university. But at the same time, I had the horrible feeling it would have been better if he hadn't come—if they'd gone ahead and dunked me. At least it would be over with. I knew Denise wouldn't let me off so easily, and when she found out that Les was my brother, as she surely would, she'd be all the more determined to do me in. If Les hadn't come, my hair would be smelly and the kids would tease me, but at least it would be *over*, like a dental appointment you've been dreading for months. Now I had to worry every day, forever and ever, about what Denise would think up next.

I soon found out. When I went to my locker after

school, someone had been there first. Someone had taken tissue paper from the toilet up on second and pushed it, wet and smelly, through the air slots of my locker. Crud was running down the other side, and my books and jacket smelled like sewage.

7 🌸 Bodies

THE WEEKEND couldn't come fast enough for me. Pamela and Elizabeth were glad, too. Elizabeth had stayed in the rest room so long at lunchtime that someone reported, and Elizabeth was embarrassed by the nurse knocking on the door of the toilet stall and asking if she was all right. Pamela had her nose out of joint because after all the worry about SGSD, and then her decision that it might be very *nice* to sing in front of an audience, she wasn't asked.

We rode our bikes over to the grade school on Saturday afternoon and shot baskets. I'm pretty good at basketball, even though I'm shorter than both Elizabeth and Pamela. I'm quick, too, and can jump higher than they can. Pamela's not bad, either, but Elizabeth always wants to stop as soon as she starts to sweat. So after we'd played for twenty minutes, we took off our jackets and sprawled on the school steps in the sunshine, looking out over the sidewalk where we used to play hopscotch.

There was something about coming back to the grade school that felt like going home to Grandma's —all the memories, I mean. There were the kindergarten and first-grade windows with drawings of colored leaves and pumpkins pasted on them. We could even see into the library, where the rocking chair sat in one corner, just inviting a boy or girl to curl up on its lap and read a story. We remembered how we had come out the front door for the big Halloween parade and realized that this year we weren't even going trick-or-treating.

"I didn't know how much I liked sixth grade until I left," Elizabeth said. "They never would have allowed an SGSD here, and no one would ever have had to lock herself in a toilet."

"It was more fun in sixth grade," Pamela agreed. "We got to do more. We got to go on overnight camping trips with our teachers, we got to put on a play. It was always the sixth graders people clapped for the most in the Halloween parade. Everybody paid attention to us. In seventh, no one even knows who we are. Personally, I can't wait till I'm in ninth. I already know how I'm going to wear my hair to the ninth-grade semiformal. I saw a picture of it in a magazine."

I didn't even know what color socks I was going to wear the next day, and Pamela already knew how she was going to wear her hair to a ninth-grade dance. Pamela just assumed she'd be invited. I not only wasn't sure I'd be invited, I wasn't even sure I'd be alive— not if Denise and her gang got hold of me. I guess if you have long blond hair, you think about it a lot. But if I counted up how much time I fussed over *my* hair, it would probably be thirty seconds in the morning and maybe fifteen seconds at night. Ninth grade, as far as I was concerned, was light-years away.

Elizabeth had been thinking about it, though. Ninth grade. Hair. "How?" she asked.

"The sides brought up like this," said Pamela, sweeping up the long yellow locks beside her face, "and pinned up with curls at the top and flowers tucked all around."

"Who do you suppose we'll be dating then?" Elizabeth asked. "You know, ninth grade wouldn't be so bad if we didn't have to go through seventh and eighth to get there."

"But once we graduate," I reminded them, "we'll have to start high school, and then we'll be at the bottom of the heap again."

"And after high school, there's college," said Elizabeth mournfully.

"And once we get a job, we'll be at the bottom of the ladder," Pamela added. "Maybe that's all life is, you know? Just climbing up, coming down, and starting all over again."

It was depressing, all right. We sat for a long time, looking out over the playground, and finally it was

Elizabeth who broke the silence. "Some day," she said, "we'll think back to this very day when we were sitting here talking like this, and we'll realize how wonderful it was. You know what we should do? I think we should promise each other that no matter *what* happens to us in junior high or high school, no matter how awful or embarrassing it is, we can always tell each other, and none of us will ever laugh."

"I promise," I said right off, feeling just how serious this was.

"So do I," said Pamela.

We sort of crossed arms so that all three of us were shaking hands on it at the same time, and it was like our own secret promise, just the three of us, friends forever. Through high school, anyway.

On Monday, Denise and her friends were lying low. I guess they decided that after cramming all that toilet paper through the vents in my locker, they'd made enough trouble for a while, but it didn't mean they were through with me. Not at all. A girl whose brother saves her just when the initiation is going full blast isn't going to get off the hook so easily. Not only had Lester loused up their plan, but he'd embarrassed Denise in front of the other kids who had come to watch. Denise would take it out on me. I knew it as surely as the ears on my head.

What I couldn't figure out about Denise was why she and the three girls she went around with acted like the world was against them. At first I thought maybe it was because they looked the way they did. Then I realized that there were several girls in school who were as heavy as Denise—*heavier*, even—who always seemed to have a crowd of friends around them and were always on committees and things. The reporter who interviewed me for the newspaper was short, one of the cheerleaders was tall and thin, and the president of the ninth-grade class, who led the pep assembly, had zits. So was it zits and height and weight that made a difference, or how you felt about it?

That noon in the cafeteria, something really crazy happened—not with Denise and her gang, but with a group of ninth-grade boys who had just finished eating and were leaving. We always watched the ninth-grade boys, because they seemed so much more clever and wonderful than seventh- and eighth-grade boys. They were joking around, and just after they'd passed our table, one of them yelled, "Boxer check!" And while Pamela, Elizabeth, and I stared, along with every other girl in the cafeteria, they unzipped their pants, lowered their jeans, and compared their boxer shorts to see who had the loudest, wildest underwear that day.

I positively gaped, my mouth hanging open. One boy had Mickey Mouse on his; another had zigzag stripes of pink, yellow, and purple; another had red hearts and cupids; and the fourth had Hawaiian palm trees and surfers. Everybody was standing up trying to see, clapping and cheering, and the guy with the palm trees was declared the winner. We all laughed, even the teacher on duty, the boys pulled their jeans up again, picked up their books, and went outside.

Pamela and I had our heads on the table in laughter, and when we finally got our breath and looked up, we saw Elizabeth staring straight ahead, unblinking, her face peppermint pink.

"Hey, Elizabeth," I said, waving one hand in front of her eyes.

"I can't believe it," she murmured. "I just can't believe it."

Pamela was still giggling. "Alice, can you imagine any *seventh*-grade boy doing something like that?"

No, I could not. I remembered when a boys' gym class joined ours for a day of basketball the week before. While we were all sitting on the floor getting instructions, one of the seventh-grade boys, sitting in the knee-chest position, pulled the bottom of his T-shirt down over his legs and pretended his knees were breasts poking through his shirt. Except for a boy back in third grade who stuck crayons up his nose once and pretended he was an elephant, that was the stupidest thing I'd ever seen. "Boxer check" was a whole lot more fun. But not, evidently, for Elizabeth.

"I never saw a boy in his underpants in my life except in the Sears catalog," she said, still in shock.

We didn't realize what a big deal it was for Elizabeth, though, until a few days had gone by and she was still talking about it. What if somebody called "Boxer check" and one of the boys had a hole in his shorts? she wondered. What if somebody called "Boxer check" and one of the boys wasn't wearing any shorts at all? Her imagination was working overtime.

By the end of the week, I found out why. Pamela invited us to her house for a sleepover, her parents went out to a movie, and that's when Elizabeth started talking.

I guess there's something about three girls in front of a fireplace making s'mores together that makes them feel warm and close and comfortable with each other. We were just sitting there, licking the chocolate and marshmallow off our fingers, watching the flames dance, when Elizabeth said suddenly, "Remember the other day on the playground when we promised we could tell each other secrets and nobody would laugh?"

Pamela and I nodded.

"Well ..." Elizabeth raised her shoulders and took a deep breath, then stared down at her feet. "I'm twelve years old, I'm in junior high, but I've—I've never seen a boy naked."

I was waiting for her to get to the point, then realized that *was* the point.

"So?" I said. "Elizabeth, you can still graduate."

She gulped. "You don't understand. I just feel so—so stupid. So backward and babyish and everything."

"But how *could* you see a boy naked? You don't have any brothers," I said, trying to make her feel better.

She looked at me intently. "You've seen Lester, then." I guess that's what she really wanted to know.

"Well, of course! Dad, too. ..." And then I realized I was going to have to explain. It wasn't like we all took our clothes off and paraded around. If someone took a shower, though, and went to his room to dress, he may or may not have a towel around him. It just wasn't very important in our house. But Elizabeth's face was turning peppermint again.

"Haven't you ever seen *your* dad?" I asked her.

"No!" She looked at me in horror.

"Haven't you even seen *pictures* of naked men?" Pamela asked curiously.

"*No!*" Elizabeth said indignantly. And then she looked miserable again. "Just statues and things. I mean, if those ninth-grade boys ever pulled down their *shorts*, I'd probably faint."

"No, you wouldn't," said Pamela, and now we were both looking at her, and it was Pamela's turn to blush. "Listen, I've got something to tell you, but you've got to promise, *promise*, that you won't ever tell the other kids at school."

Elizabeth promised and crossed herself. I just crossed my arms over my chest and promised, and hoped that would do.

"Well," said Pamela, "I've seen a whole lot of boys naked all at once, and it wasn't that great, believe me."

"Where?" Elizabeth and I asked together, as though we were going to get up and race right to wherever it was.

Pamela hugged herself with her arms and stared into the fire. "My parents . . ." she began, then stopped. "My parents . . ." she said again, "are nudists."

Elizabeth and I couldn't take our eyes off her. I couldn't quite believe what I'd heard.

"You mean they ...?"

Pamela nodded. "They go to a camp sometimes, and everybody takes off their clothes."

"In *front* of everyone?" Elizabeth said, aghast.

"Of course. Everybody does. They took me once on visiting day, but I decided I didn't want to join, so I didn't have to take mine off."

"What ... d-do they do ... a-after they take off their clothes?" Elizabeth stammered.

"The same things they do when they have their clothes on. Swim, play tennis, hike, sit around and talk."

"Then why ...?" I just couldn't understand.

"Because they say it feels better to be naked."

"And nobody ever ...?" I just couldn't stop. I was worse than Elizabeth.

"No. It's supposed to be bad manners to even stare at someone else. At *those* places, I mean."

I couldn't figure it out. If you only wanted to take off your clothes, you could do it at home. If you wanted to take off your clothes in front of people, you went to a nudist camp. But if you couldn't look at anybody else after they took their clothes off, then ...

But right now that wasn't my problem. Right now Pamela and Elizabeth were looking at me, because they had each confided something very personal, and it was my turn. So finally I told them about the most embarrassing moment in my life so far: how I had first met Patrick when I opened the door of the wrong dressing room at the Gap, and there stood this boy with red hair and blue underpants. Pamela and Elizabeth both squealed in embarrassment.

"But you know," I said, "I don't think it bothered Patrick much at all."

"He'd make a good nudist," said Pamela.

After we went to bed that night in the Joneses' family room, I was thinking how just a couple months ago, I'd never heard of SGSD. I didn't know that Lester was going to have to choose between Marilyn and Crystal. I didn't know that Dad was going to be caught between Janice Sherman and Helen Lake. And I certainly didn't know that Pamela's parents took off their clothes outside on weekends. What would I discover a few months from *now*? What was waiting to shock me once I was in eighth grade? In ninth? In *college*?

Saturday morning at breakfast, I couldn't help staring at Mrs. Jones as she made our waffles. She looked like an ordinary woman in an ordinary robe, but I knew better. When Pamela's father walked through the kitchen in his sweat pants and shirt to go jogging, I imagined him running through the woods without any pants at all. Maybe when you come right down to it, nobody is an "ordinary person." Maybe everyone has secrets. Janice Sherman, for example. When I put in my three hours at the Melody Inn later, I was thinking how nobody else who walked in that store would have guessed that the woman in charge of sheet music was secretly in love with her boss.

That night at dinner, I told Dad and Lester about the Joneses going to a nudist camp (I hadn't promised not to tell my family), and when neither one appeared shocked, I grew awfully quiet.

"Have *you* ever been to a nudist camp, Dad?" I asked finally.

"Nope."

"Why not?"

Dad shrugged. "Oh, I don't know. Maybe if it was back in the 1890s and we all wore tight collars and long sleeves in the summertime, I might consider it. But the way people can walk around outdoors now with hardly anything on at all—well, I just don't see the point."

If there were any secrets in my family, I wanted to find out about them now, so I turned to Lester. "Have *you* ever been to a nudist camp?"

Lester was wolfing down a big plate of ravioli.

"No," he said between bites. "Takes all the mystery out of life. I like a *little* something left to the imagination."

After dinner, I took a sack of pretzels to my room and thought about bodies. I decided that if there was one thing seventh-grade girls think about more than anything else—certainly more than boys—it's bodies. I guess it's because eighth- and ninth-grade girls have so much more body than we do, we're always wondering when the rest of ours is going to arrive. They have curves where we have angles. Our knees and elbows still look like ice picks. I couldn't wait to start feeling more like a butterfly and less like a praying mantis.

I was thinking, too, about what I could do for Elizabeth. Hadn't we promised we were friends for life? What would a real friend do? By the time my homework was done, I had a plan.

I went to the shelves in our dining room where Dad stores all our old magazines and journals, and started way back with the April 1957 issue of the *National Geographic*. I was determined to find every single photograph I could of a naked man or boy, paperclip it, and put it aside for Elizabeth.

There were about four hundred issues to go through, but I kept at it. Actually, there were only a few pictures of men from the front. Too many photographs had been taken from behind, or with the man holding a spear or shield right over the place Elizabeth most wanted to see.

By Sunday evening, the floor of the dining room was half covered with separate piles of *National Geographic*s—the best photos in one, the side views in another, the rear views in another, with paperclips strewn all over the place.

"Ye gods, Al, what the heck are you working on?" Lester asked, coming through.

"A project," I told him. "I'm almost done."

He pulled out a chair, sat down, and leaned over to look at a mountain climber on the cover of one. "Well, if your teacher knows how much time you put into this, you'll get the best grade in the class," he said.

I should have just dropped it right then, but I had to go and say, "It's not for school; it's for Elizabeth."

"You're doing all this for Elizabeth?" Lester said. "Why doesn't she look through her own magazines?" And the next thing I knew, Lester was reaching for one of the copies on top of the "best pictures" pile.

I threw myself bodily on the pile. "No!" I screamed. "Don't look."

Lester stared down at me. Dad came in from the kitchen where he was making chili.

"What kind of project is this, Al?" Lester said, picking up a magazine from the "side view" pile instead, noticing the paperclip, and turning right to it. I wriggled under the table on my stomach and buried my head in my arms. "New Guinea?" Lester said after a minute. When I didn't answer, he picked up another magazine and found the paperclip. "Australia?" he asked, then reached for another. "The Amazon?" There was a long, long pause. "I'll be a son of a gun," he said at last.

I didn't want him making fun of Elizabeth. Not after all we'd shared and confided and promised. I sat up so fast I bumped my head on the table.

"She's never seen a naked man in her life, and I'm just trying to help!" I bellowed.

"Well, for crying out loud," said Lester, and went on

flipping through the magazines. Then he shook his head. "Elizabeth sure isn't going to learn very much this way."

Suddenly I thought about those magazines that had pictures of naked women in them, the kind on sale in drugstores, and wondered if there were magazines with naked men in them. Lester should know.

"Lester," I said. "Would you be willing to do a big, big favor for Elizabeth?"

Lester leaped up out of the chair. "Are you crazy? No way! You're *nuts!*"

"Oh, not that," I said. "All I want you to do is buy a magazine with naked men in them so Elizabeth can see what they really look like without spears in the way."

Now Dad was in the room. "Al," he said. "You don't need those kinds of magazines, and we can certainly do better than *National Geographics.*"

"We can?"

"Tomorrow after school," he said. "Meet me at the Melody Inn. We've got a date."

Every so often, Dad does that. Gets mysterious. I didn't say anything to Elizabeth and Pamela, but when I got to the Melody Inn after school the next day, Dad already had his suit coat on and came right out when he saw me.

"Where are we going?" I asked, grabbing his arm as we crossed Georgia Avenue. "Are we walking or driving?"

"Walking."

"Will we be inside or outside?"

"Inside."

"Do we pay or is it free?"

"Free."

"Can we get something to eat while we're at it?"

"Afterward, maybe."

I couldn't imagine. The YMCA locker room, perhaps? But when we turned up the walk of the Silver Spring Library, I skidded to a stop. "Oh, no!" I said. "I'm not going in there and asking for pictures of naked men. No way."

"Relax," said Dad. "You're a big girl now."

I followed him in and over to the microfische file. "What do I look up?" I murmured. " 'Men, naked'?"

"How about 'human body'?" said Dad.

I tried that, but got human biology instead, and there were a lot of listings under 612.6. I walked around the room until I found the shelves of 612 books, and then, while Dad read the *New York Times*, I sat down on the floor and looked at books on the human body. Books on sex, I discovered, were in the same section.

I was absolutely, positively, amazed. Dad was right. I didn't have to buy magazines from the drugstore or look through four hundred copies of the *National Geographic*. There were pictures, all right. I don't mean diagrams with all the insides showing—the heart in blue and the lungs in red and the liver in green or yellow. These were drawings so real they were like photographs of everything you could possibly want to see, and things you didn't even know about yet. Skin and hair drawings of what boys look like when they are six, ten, fourteen, and twenty. There were even real photographs of a woman having a baby. Someday I'd show those to Elizabeth, but one thing at a time, I decided.

A librarian came by to get a book from the shelf, and she couldn't help but see what I was looking at; she didn't even blink. Like it was okay to be curious. I felt almost the way I did at the grade school the other day. Safe. Protected.

When I picked out four books for Elizabeth, the man at the checkout desk didn't stare at me or anything, either. He checked out my books on bodies as casually as if I were reading up on the Civil War or photosynthesis or how to build a bird feeder. I had to know if this was just an act or if librarians were always glad to have you read stuff. So just before we left the library, I went over to a woman at the reference desk and asked where I would find a list of nudist camps.

It wasn't just an act, it was real. "I think those would be listed under sunbathers in our directory of associations," she said, without batting an eye. She reached for a large book. "Let me check."

"Oh, I don't need to know right now. I just wondered where to look," I told her. "Thanks a lot."

I smiled and she smiled, but what I didn't realize was that Dad was waiting for me by the door and heard everything I said.

"Al?" he said curiously as we went outside.

I grinned. "Relax," I said. "I'm a big girl now."

When I showed the books to Elizabeth later, she said she would be grateful forever. She didn't know, either, that you could find out anything at all at a library—*those* kinds of things, I mean.

Well, almost everything. I knew that libraries had books about friendship and novels about bullies, but there wasn't any book exactly titled *How to Get Along with Denise Whitlock*. There were some problems, I discovered in the days to come, that you had to work out for yourself.

8 ✿ *The Frog Stand*

JUNIOR HIGH sure has a way of mixing you up, tossing kids around like a giant blender. I didn't have any classes at all with Pamela. I had World Studies with Patrick, P.E. with Elizabeth, and Language Arts *and* Phys. Ed. with Denise Whitlock.

Why couldn't I have had no classes at all with Denise, and Language Arts and P.E. with Pamela? Was it pure luck, or did someone in the school office decide on each pupil individually, moving him or her about from square to square like a game of Monopoly?

Elizabeth said that everything that happens to us is part of God's plan for the universe. I said that God must have a terrific sense of humor, but I still didn't know why I was the girl that Denise Whitlock most liked to kick around. I didn't think God could hate me that much. Except for Language Arts, where I sat right behind her, I tried to avoid Denise whenever I could. But she did everything possible to embarrass me in P.E.

Right at that particular moment, I couldn't see any way that P.E. would be helpful to me. I couldn't see the importance of school in general, if you want the truth. Not *my* classes, anyway. I used to think that math was one of the most useless subjects, because I had to figure out things like what was 17 percent of a gross of pencils, and I can guarantee that I will go my whole life never having to know the answer to that.

Then I wondered if World Studies wasn't even less helpful than math. Where would I ever go that I would be ashamed if I couldn't define Alexander II's Act of Emancipation of 1861? In Language Arts, would the world really end if I didn't know everything there was about predicates? I don't think Miss Summers liked predicates any more than I did. I always felt that her heart was in poetry or stories, and that she only taught us grammar because she had to. Home economics was probably the most useful subject except that I already knew how to cook the things I like best and didn't care whether I ever learned to cook liver and Brussels sprouts or not.

"You're missing the point, Al," Dad said when I complained to him about all my useless subjects. "You may not need to know what 17 percent of a gross is, but there will be plenty of times you'll need to know a certain percentage of something. You just need to learn how to apply these things to other problems, that's all."

I didn't answer.

"Sometimes," Dad went on, "when we're upset about one part of something—school, for example—we feel angry about it all."

When I still didn't answer, he said, "So what's up?"

"P.E.," I told him, slinging the plates into the cupboard like I was dealing cards. "When you were in junior high, Dad, can you remember what you had to do in P.E.?"

Dad finished wiping off the top of the stove. "Oh, baseball, basketball—maybe a little wrestling. Track."

"Do you know what *we* have to learn this grading period?" I told him. "The ring swing, the rope climb, the wall kick, and the frog stand."

"Oh," said Dad. "Well, that explains it."

The rings I liked fine, actually. You grabbed hold of a ring hanging by a long rope from the ceiling, got a running start, and swung yourself over to the next ring, which was a little higher off the floor. Then you pumped your legs back and forth until you reached the next ring and the next, before you worked your way back down again. But useful? If I were ever in a jungle and had to cross a swamp with alligators in it, and there were grapevines handy, I suppose the ring swing would be good to know.

I could also understand having to know how to climb up to the ceiling and down again on a knotted rope in case I was ever on the tenth floor of a burning hotel and had to lower myself by bed sheets.

But the wall kick and the frog stand must have been thought up by some troll who lives in the school broom closet.

"The wall kick," said the instructor, standing before us in shorts and T-shirt, "helps strengthen the thigh and calf muscles, and requires a certain agility that takes a bit of practice. But that's the name of the game, girls. Practice." And then she demonstrated.

Standing twenty feet back from the cinderblock wall, the instructor charged like she was going to throw herself right through it, then leaped up against the wall with her left foot and, bringing her right foot over her left leg, jumped down onto the mat again facing us, back to the wall. It looked so easy.

"What you're doing," she said, "is using your left leg as a yardstick, and jumping over it."

What we were doing, in case she didn't know, was the second stupidist thing we would ever be asked to do in P.E. all semester. The only use I could see for it was if we were running across a field at night and suddenly came to a barn. If we knew the wall kick, I guess, we could keep from crashing into it by leaping up on it with our left foot and turning ourselves around. But the first most stupid thing we had to do in P.E. in seventh grade was the frog stand, and I couldn't think of anything useful for that at all.

The hardest part was not laughing when the instructor demonstrated. She squatted down, knees poking out to the sides, arms between her knees, hands flat on the floor. Then she tilted her body forward, bracing her arms against the insides of her knees, until her feet were off the floor and her whole body was balanced on the palms of her hands. That would be useful, I suppose, if I were a frog in the process of laying eggs.

"Why can't they teach us something important, Dad?" I asked, following him into the living room. "Like how to walk like a model or dance the mambo or something I'll want to know in high school?"

"I'd settle for teaching girls how to climb a ladder and clean out the gutters," Dad said, trying a new song on the piano.

It was because Dad was playing the piano that he didn't hear the phone ring, so I answered. It was Aunt Sally.

"Alice, dear, I've been so curious to know how things came out with that Sherman woman and the girl your father met on the beach," she said.

I didn't want to go into the whole business of what happened, so I just said that Janice Sherman wasn't bothering Dad anymore and that Helen Lake would be coming to Washington soon to visit.

"That's wonderful!" said Aunt Sally. "So he's in love, then."

"Well, sort of," I told her. "I can't really say." And then, because I had her on the phone, I asked, "Aunt Sally, what did you have to do in P.E. back in seventh grade?"

"What's P.E.?"

"Physical Education."

"Oh, *gym*, you mean. Well, we had to wear heavy blue cotton dresses with short skirts and snaps down the front, and matching panties with tight elastic around the legs. I remember that," she said. "They were perfectly dreadful."

I could imagine. "But what did you have to *do*?"

There was silence. "You know, Alice," Aunt Sally said. "All I actually remember about gym class is that a woman was hired to play the piano while we did our exercises. We had an instructor who believed that if we did anything more strenuous than that, our wombs would drop or something. So we ran around in huge circles flapping our arms in time to the music—'*Leap*, run, run. . . . *Leap*, run, run.' That was even worse than the gym suits."

I agreed.

"Mostly," said Aunt Sally, "I spent my seventh grade in mortal terror because there was a rumor that sometime during the year, the eighth-grade boys descended on the seventh-grade girls' dressing room and nobody could stop them. They'd go on a rampage, stealing bras and panties and things, and we were always afraid they were going to come roaring through while we were naked. They never did."

I stood listening with my mouth half open. Way back in Aunt Sally's time, then—when Moses was alive, practically—there were initiations, ceremonies, that scared you to death.

"*Had* they ever really done it?" I asked her.

"Everybody *said* they had, but I never met anyone who had actually seen it happen. But Alice, I was so shy and so scared that I always dressed and undressed in a curtain."

"A *curtain?*"

Aunt Sally gave an embarrassed laugh. "The dressing room was divided into tiny cubicles, and each cubicle had a heavy white curtain in front of it. I would always wrap the curtain around me, sort of hold it closed with my chin, and take off my clothes inside it, so that if the eighth-grade boys came running through, I could hold the curtain tight and they wouldn't see anything."

I think I understood Aunt Sally a little better after that.

We were soon going to be tested on the four exercises in P.E., though. The teacher had already told us that in order to get a C for the grading period, each girl had to pass three out of four. Elizabeth, Pamela, and I were really scared we might not make that C. We'd mastered the ring swing and the rope climb, but we'd given up completely on the wall kick. That left only the frog stand to see us through.

I invited the girls over one afternoon to practice. We pushed the folding table against the wall in the dining room, and then, one at a time, squatted down and tried balancing on our hands while the other two girls gave pointers.

Surprisingly, I was the one who got it first. It's sort

of like learning to ride a bike, I guess. First you tip too far one way, and then you tip too far the other, and finally you learn what you have to do to be perfectly balanced, and after you get the feel of it, it's not so hard.

"Croak!" I said, squatting there with my rear end and heels off the floor.

Pamela got it next. She teetered back and forth a couple of times, and then, there she was, heels up, her weight resting on her hands. "Croak, croak!" said Pamela.

But Elizabeth just couldn't get it. She was either tipping forward, landing on her head, or tipping backward, landing on her rear. Even when Pamela and I steadied her from either side, like training wheels, Elizabeth went down the minute we let go. She collapsed in tears.

"I just can't *do* it!" she sobbed.

"Elizabeth, relax," I said. "Maybe you're trying too hard."

"I'm going to fail gym!" she wailed. "They can keep me in every day after school for a year, but I'll never be able to do it. My body's unbalanced or something."

We tried explaining to her that everybody has a different center of gravity, and one way or another, she'd find what was right for her. Elizabeth went on bawling.

"W-when you go on to high school and I'm still back in seventh grade, will you come visit me?" she wept.

"Blow your nose, Elizabeth, and try it some more," I said. "Remember when you first learned to ride a bike or skate? Once you got it, you got it. It'll happen."

And it did, about fifteen minutes later. Just after Pamela had mastered the art of not only balancing but of taking a few steps on her hands, Elizabeth shrieked that she had done it, only to fall over on her nose. But she tried again, balanced again, and once she knew what it felt like, she did it a third time and a fourth.

"Croak!" said Elizabeth happily.

"Croak! Croak!" I said, balancing beside her.

"Croak, croak, croak!" said Pamela, waddling around the dining room, her rear end bobbing up and down.

Suddenly we all froze, because there in the hallway was Lester, jacket in his hand.

"Don't tell me, let me guess," he said, closing the door behind him.

Elizabeth promptly gave a little squeal that sounded like air going out of a tire, and fell over on her side. Pamela shrieked and fell backward.

"A handsome prince came by to kiss you, and this is what happened," Lester said.

Before I could explain, Elizabeth and Pamela had rolled across the floor toward the kitchen, stumbled to their feet, and locked themselves in the pantry.

A pantry, I found out when we first moved into this house, is a little closet off the kitchen, where cooks used to store their food.

"We're practicing the frog stand for P.E.," I told Lester, "and we finally got it."

"Shall I open a bottle of champagne or something?" he said, and went right out to the kitchen.

"What are you doing?" I asked, knowing that Elizabeth and Pamela wouldn't come out until he left.

"Making myself some lunch," he said. "I had a one o'clock exam this afternoon and haven't had anything since breakfast."

I figured he'd put a pizza in the microwave, take it upstairs, and turn on his stereo. Instead, he opened the refrigerator door and stood there, talking out loud to himself. "Shall I make eggs Benedict," he said, "or boil some pasta? The pasta's quickest, but ... naw. Why don't I go all out and make pancakes from scratch. Blueberry pancakes. I'll have to thaw the blueberries in hot water, but I could get the griddle going, and ..."

Suddenly the door to the pantry flew open and, like marathon runners, Elizabeth and Pamela bolted to the front hall, their faces red as Santa's britches. I ran after them as far as the porch.

"Tell Lester I will never forgive him as long as I live," said Pamela. "He just did that on purpose."

I went back inside. "Pamela says she will never forgive you as long as she lives," I repeated.

"Good," said Lester.

On the day of the test, the P.E. instructor walked along the girls seated on the floor, drawing imaginary lines between groups and naming each one: "Group A here, Group B, Group C over here, and Group D."

She took four clipboards and handed one to each group. "I want you to grade yourselves on the four exercises we've been learning. Each girl, for each exercise, should receive either a pass or fail, and after class, I want to see each girl who did not pass at least three."

I was glad I hadn't happened to be sitting next to Denise Whitlock and two of her friends. They were all in the same group, though, and I knew right off they'd pass each other whether they could do the exercises or not. It wasn't fair.

I didn't know any of the girls in my group except Elizabeth. I think most of them were eighth and ninth graders, and one of them had done the wall kick perfectly the first time she tried it. I felt like an elephant in a field with deer. But I passed the three I expected to, and then, when our group finished early, we sat watching the girls in the other groups.

It really made me angry the way Denise and her friends were passing each other. Denise only made it halfway up the rope climb, but her friends wrote "pass" beside her name. She couldn't do the frog stand, either, not for more than half a second, but they passed her on that, too. When she went to do the wall kick, she went lumbering toward the cinderblock wall, got one foot only a few inches up, stumbled over it with her other foot, and landed on her stomach with a loud "Oof!"

I saw a number of girls smile, but I was the only one who laughed. I couldn't help it. It wasn't a loud laugh, not a long laugh, but a quick chortle of pure delight.

Every dog has its day, a line came to me. Now where

had I heard that before? From Aunt Sally? Something my own mother used to say?

When Denise got her breath back, she sat down and wouldn't try it again. The instructor came over to be sure she was okay. I pressed my lips together to stop the smiling. It was worth the ring swing, the rope climb, the wall kick, and the frog stand just to see Denise fall flat on her stomach. It was worth all the torture of the past few weeks just to hear that "Oof" when she landed.

When I was in the shower later, though, I didn't feel that good about it anymore, because the feud with Denise Whitlock stood in the way of my goal for seventh grade. So far I got along with all my teachers, even Mr. Hensley. I hadn't had any quarrels with Pamela or Elizabeth, and Patrick and I were still good friends. I could honestly say that I was on good terms with everyone in junior high school except for Denise Whitlock and her gang.

I wished that whatever problems you had could be washed away in a hot shower. Too fat? Too skinny? Too tall? Too short? Too loud? Too shy? Just step in the magic shower, turn on the water, and you'd come out perfect.

I'd been in there longer than I should have, so I quickly turned the water off and reached for my towel. My fingers felt along the shower rod but didn't find it. I moved the curtain aside to see if it had fallen on the floor. It wasn't there. I knew without asking that Denise and her friends had come by while I was in there and made off with my towel.

I was late already, but I had to come out of the shower naked, go out into the dressing area in front of all the other girls who were standing outside their cubicles now, pulling on their jeans and tying their sneakers. I had to go back up to the towel desk and ask for another.

A piercing wolf whistle rattled the windows of the dressing area, and I heard some girls laugh. I knew it wasn't eighth-grade boys coming in for a raid, but I almost wished it was. I'd simply roll myself up in a dressing room curtain the way Aunt Sally used to do and let them come. But there was nothing to roll up in to protect myself from Denise, and the war went on and on.

9 ❀ *Mother Alice*

ON WEDNESDAY, Lester was really sick. I went over to Pamela's for a couple hours after school, and when I got home, Lester was lying on the couch, one arm dangling off the side, his fingers curled on the rug.

"You cooking tonight or am I?" I asked. When he didn't answer, I walked over to see if he was breathing.

"Pizza," I said in his ear. "Hot pepperoni pizza dripping with cheese."

His back was moving up and down, but he still didn't open his eyes.

"Ice cold Coca Cola," I said, six inches from his face.

He didn't budge.

"Marilyn in a bikini."

When he gave no sign that he was even conscious, I put one hand on his forehead. It was warm as cocoa.

For the first time in my life, I was worried about Lester. *Really* worried, I mean. He wasn't sick very often, and then it was usually only a cold. I guess I figured that because he was eight years older than I, he could take care of himself. Now he couldn't even open his eyes.

I shook his arm. "Lester? You okay?"

"Unngghh," he said finally, his mouth half buried in the couch cushion.

"Les," I said, "you're burning up."

He licked at his lips. I kept pestering him, shaking his arm until he finally opened one eye.

"Should I call Dad? You're really sick."

He rolled over on his side and put one hand on his throat. "It's sore," he said.

"You ought to be in bed," I told him.

He tried to sit up, then fell back. "I've got a date with Marilyn. What time is it?"

"Time for you to see a doctor, Les. I'm worried. Feel your *head*!"

"I'm okay," he said, but his voice was raspy. "Go call the cleaners, will you, and see if my shirts came back?"

I went to the phone and called Dad. He said he'd be home in fifteen minutes, not to let Lester out of the house, and that he didn't have the brains of a cocker spaniel.

I imagined having to put my bicycle chain around one of Lester's ankles and padlock him to the sofa, but it wasn't necessary. When I came back in the room, he was on his stomach again, eyes closed, and didn't even speak.

When Dad came home, Lester's forehead felt even hotter.

"Help me get him on his feet and out to the car, Al," Dad said. "I'm going to drive him to the emergency room at Holy Cross."

We pulled Lester into a sitting position, then Dad knelt down and put one of Lester's arms around his neck, hoisting him up on his feet. I braced his other side. I felt like a sandbag holding back the Mississippi. We sort of dragged Les out the front door, down the steps, and plopped him in the back seat of the car.

Lester opened his eyes halfway. "You get my shirts, Al?" he asked.

"Les, you're going to the hospital," Dad said. "Al, call Marilyn and tell her Lester's sick and can't possibly take her out. I'll call you from the emergency room as soon as we know what's what."

I nodded, watched the car drive off, then went back inside and sat down on the couch, in the very spot where Lester had been lying. The cushions were still warm. I wondered what I'd do if anything happened to my brother. I didn't know how much I needed him until I thought of never having him around again. Why was it I had to wait till something like this happened to think of all the ways I'd been a horrible sister?

I remembered the time Dad bought a fancy cake for

Lester's birthday. He put it on a platter, and all the while he was making supper, I was nibbling the frosting off the sides. If anyone should have eaten the icing off the sides, it was Les because it was his birthday.

Just when I decided I hadn't done anything more awful than that, I remembered how I'd taken one of his sweaters, without asking, to wear on a field trip and lost it. And as long as I'd been making supper, I'd given Lester the worst of everything. If there was mold on the bread when I made sandwiches, I'd pinch it off and give that slice to Lester. *I* certainly didn't want to eat it, and I wouldn't think of giving it to Dad. If there was wilted lettuce, it always went in Lester's salad bowl, not mine or Dad's. Once I even dropped a hamburger pattie on the floor when I was taking it off the stove. I wiped it with my hand and put it on Lester's bun. He never knew. It was as though he was a garbage disposal or something.

It wasn't until the phone rang that I remembered I was supposed to call Marilyn and tell her what had happened. It was probably Marilyn calling Lester, wondering where he was.

I stumbled over my feet on the way to the phone. It was Crystal Harkins.

"Hi, Alice," she said in her silky low voice. "How are you?"

"Okay," I told her.

"Is Les there?"

I was so glad I could tell her the truth and didn't have to say he was with Marilyn that I just warbled it out: "He's awfully sick, Crystal. Dad's taken him to the emergency room."

"Oh, Alice! What's wrong with him?"

"I'm not sure, but he's got a fever. Dad's pretty worried."

"And you're there all by yourself?"

"Dad said he'd call as soon as he found out anything."

"I'm coming over," said Crystal, and the phone clicked.

I stared at the receiver in my hand and slowly hung up. What had I done? What was I supposed to have said? I looked up Marilyn's number in the phone book and dialed.

Marilyn sounded impatient when she answered. "Hello?" Lester was late, all right.

"Marilyn, this is Alice."

Her voice grew a little softer. "Alice, where in the world is your brother? We had a reservation for dinner a half hour ago."

"He's at the hospital," I told her. "He's practically delirious, Marilyn. He kept saying he had to get over to your place, but Dad told me to call and tell you what happened."

"Good heavens! What's wrong?"

"We don't know. Dad said he'd call as soon as they found out anything."

"You'll let me know, won't you, Alice? As soon as you hear?"

"I'll call you right away," I promised.

When I hung up, I let out my breath and realized I hadn't had any dinner myself, so I went out in the kitchen and opened a can of beans and franks. When I don't have to cook for anyone else, I eat them cold out of the can. I was sitting on the couch, holding the can on my knees and watching television, when Dad called.

"Al, the doctor thinks it's strep. He's taken a throat culture and given him a shot of penicillin, but we have to wait around for a couple more tests before we come home. Did you get hold of Marilyn?"

"Yes."

"Good. You go ahead and eat, and I'll get my own supper when I get back with Les."

No sooner had I put the phone down than the door-bell rang. How was I supposed to call Marilyn and tell her what Dad said with Crystal sitting right here? I opened the front door. It was Marilyn.

"Alice, I couldn't wait. I wanted to be here when your dad calls. I'm just so worried about Les."

"Dad just called and ..." I'd only opened the door halfway, but Marilyn came right in.

"He did?" She took off her sweater. "What did he say?"

"The doctor thinks it's strep, and as soon as they take more tests, Dad's bringing Lester home."

"Then I'm so glad I came," Marilyn said, sitting down. "I want to be here when Les walks in."

I swallowed, but before I had time to say a word, I

heard the slam of a car door outside and footsteps on the porch. The doorbell rang. I tried not to look at Marilyn as I opened the door.

"Well, I'm here!" Crystal said, and walked inside.

Marilyn and Crystal stared at each other like two strange dogs. I wondered if they had ever met. Probably not.

"Um ... Crystal, this is Marilyn," I said, then wondered if it should have been the other way around. Did you introduce the person who was sitting down to the person who was standing up, or the person who was standing up to the person sitting down, or ...?

"I didn't know you had company," said Crystal.

"I'm waiting for Les," Marilyn told her.

"What a coincidence," said Crystal. "So am I."

"Sort of like a welcoming committee!" I chirped brightly. Marilyn and Crystal looked at me, but no one smiled.

Crystal chose a chair off to one side and sat down. I picked up my can off the coffee table.

"Beans and franks?" I offered.

Marilyn and Crystal shook their heads.

If I had a mother, she would have known what to do. I could have just watched and listened, and wouldn't have had to say anything. Now I had to do it all. I tried to imagine what Elizabeth's mother would do if she were here. So I sat down on a chair between the couch where Marilyn was sitting and the chair with Crystal in it and folded my hands in my lap.

"How are things at your house?" I asked Marilyn.

She was examining a chipped fingernail. "Very well, thank you," she said.

I smiled pleasantly at Crystal. "How are things at the university?"

"Couldn't be better," said Crystal. She and Marilyn exchanged stony glances.

"I think you should know, Crystal, that Les and I were going out tonight," Marilyn said at last.

"Well, I saw him at lunch, and he looked fine to me," said Crystal. "Strange he could become this sick so quickly."

"Are you suggesting—"

"It was such a beautiful day," I said quickly. "Dad calls it Indian summer."

"Are you suggesting that Les isn't really sick?" Marilyn said, ignoring me completely. I could have been a doorknob for all the attention they paid to me.

"I'm just saying that sometimes our bodies tell us what we really want to do," Crystal told her.

"I've known Les for a long time," said Marilyn.

"Then why didn't you hang on to him?" Crystal snapped. "You let him go, and as soon as he found happiness with someone else, you suddenly decided you wanted him back."

"I never stopped loving him," said Marilyn.

I could see that they could carry on a conversation quite well without me, so I picked up my can of beans and franks again and polished it off. I even forgot myself and burped, then said, "Excuse me." They looked my way, both of them startled to discover I was still in the room.

And then I heard Dad's car coming up the drive. I heard the door open and close, footsteps on the driveway, then on the steps. Crystal stood up, but Marilyn stayed where she was.

The door opened and Lester staggered in, Dad right behind him, one hand on his arm. When Les saw Crystal he came to a dead stop. Like the trunk of a tree, he stood rooted to the floor, but the top of him swayed slightly. He blinked, trying to keep his eyes open.

"Lester, you must feel awful!" Crystal said sympathetically.

Then Marilyn got up and came out in the hallway. Lester took one look at her and fell back against Dad. "I feel awful," he said.

I just looked helplessly at Dad, lifted my arms, and dropped them again. He took in the situation at a glance.

"Ladies," he said, "I have a very sick young man here who needs to get to bed."

"If there's anything I can do, Mr. McKinley—" Crystal began.

"If there's anything to be done for Lester, I'll do it," said Marilyn.

"I appreciate it," Dad said to both at once. "And I'll certainly let you know."

"It's really okay about this evening, Les," Marilyn told him. "I'll call you tomorrow, okay?"

"Okay," said Lester, only he said it to Crystal instead of Marilyn. Then he realized his mistake, turned around, and said, "Okay," again. To me.

Both girls left, and I helped Dad get Lester upstairs and in bed.

"You want me to make you some supper, Dad?" I asked.

"Tell you what. I'll get my own if you'll take a washcloth and basin and rub down Lester's arms and chest and face. It'll help lower his temperature."

"Sure," I said.

I don't know if Lester even realized who was taking care of him. When I put the washcloth on his chest, he said, "It's awful cold, Marilyn." But when I got up to add some warm water to the pan, he said, "Would you bring me a drink, Crystal?"

When I went downstairs to get him some ginger ale, I thought I heard voices outside, so I went to the window in the dark to look out. I couldn't believe it. Marilyn and Crystal were sitting on the steps, facing each other, talking. Their voices were soft and serious.

I got the ginger ale and a straw and bent it so that Lester could drink. Then I took it upstairs and sat by his bed. I didn't tell him who was sitting on the porch.

Lester looked like he might be feeling just a little better. His face was still pink with fever, but his eyes were brighter. They actually focused on me as I put the straw between his lips.

"You get my shirts?" he asked.

"Your shirts are still at the cleaners, Lester. You won't need them for a while."

"Did you call Marilyn for me?"

"Yes. She understands."

"Good," said Lester, and closed his eyes.

I think he slept while I went on bathing his chest and arms. When he opened his eyes again he said, "I dreamed that Marilyn and Cyrstal both came to see me."

I didn't think I ought to tell him that not only had they come, but they were both here together, and that if he thought he had problems now, they were nothing compared to what he'd face once he got well.

I stayed with Lester until almost nine, then took his glass back down. Dad had stretched out on the couch and was sound asleep. The front steps were empty now. Both Marilyn and Crystal had gone, and Lester was upstairs sleeping like a baby.

If there was a mother in our family, I wondered what she'd do next. I decided she would lock the doors, put a light blanket over Dad, turn out the lights, and go to bed. So I did.

10 ❀ *The Trouble with Hensley*

I WAS wrong about most of the things that might happen in Mr. Hensley's class. His breath still smelled, and he still showered the first row with spittle while he talked. But being the first person in the first row wasn't so bad, because I was first out the door when the bell rang, for one thing. And for another, Mr. Hensley never embarrassed anyone if he could help it.

"Alice," he'd say, "there were two revolutions in Russia in 1917. Can you tell me what started the first one?"

If I couldn't, or my answer was wrong, he wouldn't remind me how many questions I'd missed that week, or ask why I wasn't studying harder. He'd just go right on to Barbara, then Chris, then David or Heather, so that finally I wasn't afraid of being called on first. But

I didn't like World Studies any more than I did at the beginning, because the trouble with Hensley was that he was incredibly, stupendously, crashingly, amazingly boring.

Mr. H. is about five feet ten, squarely built, with small gray-blue eyes and grayish blond hair, and he always, *always*, wears gray or brown. Never blue. Never black. Never a single piece of clothing that has any purple, green, or yellow in it. Patrick and I were talking about it once, and he said that if Hensley ever came to class in a red sweater, the students would pass out from shock.

Not only did Mr. Hensley *look* boring, he *sounded* boring. His voice rose just a little at the beginning of each sentence and slid down to a half whisper at the end. Every sentence. He never raised his voice in anger, either. If someone wasn't paying attention, Hensley just stopped talking until the room was quiet again.

He didn't read his lectures, but it sounded as though he'd memorized them, and I figured that Mr. Hensley had probably been giving the same talks on the same days for the last twenty years. I think he was sick of them himself.

Patrick and I had begun making up little jokes about Hensley after we left class each day.

"What do you think he eats for breakfast?" I asked once.

"Cream of Wheat," Patrick said. "What do you think he does on weekends?"

"Collects rocks," I answered. "What do you suppose he reads?"

"The Economic Policy of Latvia," said Patrick. Patrick always had better answers than I did because he's traveled all over the world.

What we couldn't figure out was whether Mr. Hensley *knew* he was boring. He wore a wedding ring, so he must have a wife who should have told him just how boring he was. But then we decided that maybe his wife was as boring as he was. Maybe she wore gray dresses and gray shoes, served boring meals, raised boring children, and they all sat at intersections counting cars for excitement.

Anyway, Patrick and I made World Studies just a little more fun by sending notes back and forth. Patrick sat in the third row exactly two seats behind mine next to the door. He'd wait until Hensley had paced down to the windows on the other side of the room, and then he'd fold up a cartoon he'd drawn and slide it up the floor to my desk. I'd pick it up when Hensley wasn't looking, smile at the drawing, add a little something of my own, and slide it back. It sure made the forty minutes go faster.

Patrick was a good artist. He always drew Hensley at the front of the room. Sometimes Mr. H. looked as though he were sleepwalking, with a long string of Zs coming from his mouth. Sometimes all the students in the cartoon were yawning. Once Patrick drew two pictures side by side. One said "boar" and showed a picture of a wild pig; the other said "bore" and was, of course, Hensley.

This was about the only thing that was fun in Hensley's class. You'd think that studying about a revolution could be exciting, but Hensley managed to take out every little bit of excitement he could.

We didn't bother anyone else, unless it was Connie, the girl who sat right behind me. Connie believed in paying attention no matter what, and she always gave a disgusted sigh when a note sailed by her desk on the way to mine. But at least she never told on us or tried to pick it up.

And then something happened. On the fifth of November, Patrick drew a cartoon of Hensley in front of the class with droplets of spit coming out of his mouth, showering the kids in the first row. I grinned when I saw it, and as Mr. Hensley paced back and forth in front of the blackboard, talking about the Bolsheviks, I took Patrick's cartoon and drew umbrellas over the heads of all the kids in the first row. Then I slid it back to Patrick.

I leaned my head in my hand and tried really hard to concentrate on what Mr. Hensley was saying. The trouble was that I didn't care at all about Bolsheviks or Petrograd or even very much about revolutions, not the way Hensley teaches, anyway. He had just walked over to the window again, talking to the trees outside, it seemed, not to us, when suddenly I heard Connie gasp. I blinked and lifted my head.

"Oh, no!" I heard Patrick whisper.

I couldn't figure out what was wrong. And then I saw that the little piece of paper had skidded too far this time, and instead of stopping at my desk, had kept going three feet farther. It was lying directly in Mr. Hensley's path, and now he was coming right toward it.

He kept walking until he touched it with the toe of his shoe and then, without pausing once in his lecture, reached down, picked it up, and unfolded it there at the front of the room, all the while talking about Lenin and Alexander Kerensky.

"See?" Connie whispered over my shoulder.

I didn't even move. Mr. Hensley's voice sort of faded out, and for five seconds or so, he stared at the cartoon in his hands. He didn't look at us, didn't say anything, just stuck the paper in his pocket and went on telling about why Leon Trotsky was arrested. But his face went from gray to a faint shade of pink.

It was Patrick and I who were upset. As soon as the bell rang and we got outside, I grabbed his arm. "What did you draw on it?" I asked. "Do you think he knows it was him in the cartoon?"

Patrick swallowed. "He knows," he said, and looked miserable. "I drew wavy lines coming out of his mouth and put a sweatshirt on him that said, 'Bad Breath Hensley.'"

I moaned.

"I feel awful," said Patrick.

"So do I."

We separated for our next class, but for the rest of the day, I knew that Patrick felt as bad as I did. Patrick and I had never meant for Mr. Hensley to see those cartoons. We never showed them to anybody else. It was just a private joke between us.

I didn't have much to say that night while Dad and Lester made dinner. Dad was fixing the salad, and Les and I were making "Pots of Gold," which is cubes of cheese rolled up in Bisquick and boiled in tomato soup until they're cooked. I did the mixing and rolling and Lester did the boiling.

"*Watch* it, Al!" he said, after a minute. "Wait until these are done before you add any more. Can't you see the pot's full?" Dad says that the only thing worse than Pots of Gold is canned macaroni, but he's willing to eat it every six weeks or so because Les and I like it. Les and I like it because it's about as easy to make as canned macaroni.

"Something wrong, Al?" Dad asked. "Have hardly heard a peep out of you since I got home."

"I just feel lousy," I told him.

"Not coming down with the same thing Les had, are you?"

"Not that kind of lousy," I said, and explained what Patrick and I had done. "I mean, you can't really change if you're boring, can you?"

"Not easily," said Dad.

"That's why I feel so awful," I told him. "But it's not the kind of thing you can apologize for without embarrassing him more."

Dad agreed. "There are some things that are hard to put back in the bottle, aren't there?"

I dropped more dumplings in the tomato soup.

"How do you know he's sure you and Patrick did it?" Les asked.

"It doesn't *matter*!" I snapped. "He's embarrassed, and *we* did it, and I feel like rotten eggs."

"Well, maybe you can think of something to do to make it up to him," Dad suggested.

"Yeah, tell him you really enjoy his bad breath and his spit," Lester joked.

It wasn't funny. I sat at the table cutting each little ball of Bisquick in two with my fork, watching the melted cheese spill out. Usually this is my favorite part of the meal. But this time, it was like stabbing Mr. Hensley in the heart.

Patrick called about seven and wanted to know if he could come over. I said yes.

"Patrick, huh?" said Dad, as we cleaned up the kitchen.

"We're special friends now," I told him. Maybe that made us sound more special than what I meant, because I noticed that both Dad and Lester left us alone in the living room. Les went upstairs to watch TV, and Dad sat at the folding table in the dining room to answer some letters.

Patrick had his book bag with him. "I've got an idea," he said, and took out his notebook.

"Whatever we do, Patrick, it's not going to make him feel any better about that cartoon," I said.

"I know, but I've thought of something else." He took out the mimeographed paper of projects we were supposed to do for the unit on the Russian Revolution. "Have you signed up for any of these yet?"

I shook my head.

"Okay. Veteran's Day is Visiting Day. Right? Parents come to class."

"I thought we had Visiting Day already."

"That was Back-to-School Night. The parents came alone. This time they visit classes while we're there."

"So?"

"So all the other teachers have been getting ready. All the other classrooms have posters and papers and charts up. Right?"

I thought of Language Arts and how Miss Summers, with her Obsession perfume, had decorated the rim of the bulletin board all the way around with book jackets. Our family-tree diagrams covered an entire wall, and another wall had photographs of authors. Even the photographs smelled like perfume. Then I thought of Mr. Hensley's room. Beige walls, gray blackboard, and that's all. If you put all Mr. Hensley's imagination in a teaspoon, it wouldn't even cover the bottom.

"So let's decorate Hensley's room for him," Patrick said. "Let's sign up together for project seven."

I studied the paper in Patrick's hand. *Project Seven: Make a linear chart, marked off in years, and indicate when and where the major developments of the Russian Revolution took place, beginning with the Decembrist uprising in 1825 and ending with the for-*

*mation of the Union of Soviet Socialist Republics in
1922.*

"How is this going to brighten up the room?" I asked
doubtfully.

"Ta da!" said Patrick, and pulled out a big roll of
computer paper from his book bag. He unrolled it,
and it stretched all the way from the front door to
the kitchen sink. "We'll get it all done, decorate it
with pictures, and have it up on the wall above the
blackboard by the eleventh."

"But the projects aren't due until the twentieth!" I
protested.

"So we'll do ours early, just for him."

We worked until 10:30, just making a list of what
needed to be on the chart and marking the paper off
into years.

"I saw Patrick's bike outside your house last night,"
Elizabeth told me at the bus stop the next day.

"We're working on a history project together," I told
her.

She didn't say anything for a moment, and Pamela
was talking to some other girls. But finally Elizabeth
asked, "Did you kiss?"

"Last night? Patrick and me? No. Why?"

"I don't see how you can work side by side with
someone you used to kiss and then not do it anymore."

Sometimes it's hard to talk to Elizabeth.

I really tried to pay attention in Mr. Hensley's
class the next day. There were no more cartoons slid-

ing across the floor from Patrick's desk to mine. Mr. Hensley hadn't changed at all. He still droned on and on. He still sent out a shower of spittle when he said "Socialist" or "assassination." If he suspected that Patrick and I had drawn that cartoon, he never let on. He's too much of a gentleman to say anything that might embarrass you, even if you've embarrassed him.

Patrick came over every evening that week and spent most of the weekend at our house. We really had to work hard to make the eleventh. It wasn't easy to illustrate the Russian Revolution, but Dad said we could cut up old *National Geographics* if we found any pictures of the Soviet Union, and that helped. When we were done at last, Patrick held one end of it and I held the other, and Dad and Lester looked it over and said it was pretty good.

"*Very* good, in fact," said Dad, and made a couple of suggestions of things we'd left out. We found we could still squeeze them in. Lester even gave us a Russian kopeck from his coin collection to glue on the chart.

On Monday Patrick's dad drove us to school early. Patrick got a stepladder from the custodian, and when Hensley walked in fifteen minutes later, Patrick was up on the ladder, with half the chart taped to the wall, and I was holding the other end.

Hensley paused in the doorway, staring at us, and then walked slowly in, that faint pink in his cheeks again. I think at first he was afraid we were putting up a long cartoon about him, but when he saw what it was, his eyes lit up. It was the first time I ever saw Mr. Hensley look remotely excited.

"You're more than a week early!" he said. Then, walking slowly along the front of the room, studying the chart: "I can see you've put a lot of work into this project."

"It was fun," I told him.

He looked at me as though he had never heard the word before. I wondered if anyone else, in all Mr. Hensley's years of teaching, had ever said his class was "fun."

"You got some excellent pictures!" he said, and even his voice sounded a little excited. "Here, let me help." He took my end of the chart, stood on his desk chair, and taped it to the wall. The chart went all the way from the windows on one side of the room to the opposite side and curved three feet around one corner.

We had to leave when the first bell rang and go to homeroom, but when we came in later, there were already parents in the room, including my dad and Patrick's folks, studying the chart. I saw Mr. Hensley slip a breath mint in his mouth before he went over to talk to them, pointing out certain things on the chart, and asking Patrick and me to come up and explain others.

Maybe I only imagined it, but I swear I saw Hensley's eyes sparkle. The high point of the period, though, was when the principal came into the room briefly to see how things were going and commented on the chart. Hensley never stopped beaming for the rest of the session.

Sometimes it's possible to show you're sorry when you can't come right out and say it. It didn't change Mr. Hensley a lot. He still wore the same brown pants he always wore; his voice still droned, and he still showered the first row with spit. But he smiled more often. We noticed that.

"For two people who aren't going together anymore, you and Patrick sure have been seeing a lot of each other," Elizabeth said after school. "He was over at your house almost all weekend."

I just shrugged.

"If you don't kiss anymore, Alice, do you ever *talk* about kissing? How you used to do it, I mean?"

"Why would we talk about kissing if we don't kiss anymore?" I asked.

"Well, I mean, how can you just pretend it never happened?"

"We *don't* pretend it never happened. We just don't feel like kissing right now. We talk about other things."

"I don't see how you can possibly talk about anything else when you used to be so close that you'd put your arms around each other and your lips together and . . ."

"Elizabeth, there's more to life than kissing," I told her.

"I wouldn't know," she said, and sighed.

I guess if you've never been kissed, you think about it all the time. If Elizabeth's ever kissed, though, she's going to want a full orchestra playing, moonlight, waterfalls, the works. Boy, will she be disappointed.

11 ❀ *"Bubbles"*

I WAS really relieved that I cleared things up with Mr. Hensley. I was already on bad terms with Denise and her crowd, which messed up my goal to get through seventh grade without making a single enemy, and I sure didn't want to add a teacher to the list. What I hadn't expected, though, was that I'd soon have one of my closest friends mad at me, too. Pamela.

It was only a short while ago that we'd promised to be friends for life. And what made Pamela mad at me was no more my fault than Denise teasing me because I didn't have a mother. Another thing about seventh grade is that it isn't fair. Or maybe it's just life that's not fair.

At lunch one day in the cafeteria, Elizabeth handed

little envelopes to Pamela and me. We opened them there at the table, and we both squealed at once. Inside were pictures. Bubble-bath pictures. Last summer, on a sleepover at Elizabeth's, we had taken pictures of each other in the bathtub, covered with bubbles, and Elizabeth's mother developed the film and made prints for each of us of all three.

We promptly had a giggling fit and compared pictures, each of us covered with bubbles, only our shoulders bare. I even had bubbles on top of my head, like Martha Washington's wig or something.

After lunch period was over, I stuck my three pictures in my notebook and didn't think any more about it. Thanksgiving came, and Dad and Lester and I went to the Hot Shoppe as usual for our holiday dinner, and afterward Lester went out with Marilyn, and Crystal called to wish him Happy Thanksgiving, and I lied and said I didn't know where he was, and when Lester came home I said I'd never lie for him again so he'd better get his act together as to whether he liked Crystal or Marilyn better. By nine that night, we were all hungry again, so Lester sent out for a pizza. A typical Thanksgiving at our house.

When I went back to school on Monday, though, I was walking down the hall between first and second periods when someone I didn't even know said, "Hi, Bubbles."

"What?" I said.

Seventh-grade boys get weird sometimes, so I didn't

think much of it, but when I was in Language Arts later, two more boys called me Bubbles. "Hey, Bubbles! How ya doin'?" they said.

"What are you talking about?" I asked.

They only laughed. I began to worry that "Bubbles" was another code word like "SGSD" or something. Denise hadn't called me "Bubbles" in class, though, and if it meant something awful, she'd be the first to do it. I couldn't figure it out.

When I saw Patrick going to his locker right after lunch, I told him about it and he laughed, too.

"What's going on, Patrick?" I asked. "Do you know something I don't?"

"Maybe," he said.

I followed him down the hall to find out what it was all about, and on the inside of his locker door was the picture of me in the bubble bath, poster-size. Some boys going by whistled and grinned at me.

I stared. "Where did you *get* that?" I asked.

"Pamela gave me her picture of you, so I had a poster made," he said.

"You're nuts, Patrick," I told him, but I was a little bit pleased. It was a nice, natural, silly picture of me, and I didn't care if boys called me Bubbles. Of course, they wondered who took it and how Patrick got hold of it, but that didn't bother me, either. Everyone seemed to understand it was all a joke.

The rest of the day, when boys looked at me and yelled, "Hey, Bubbles!" I'd just laugh. Maybe seventh grade wasn't so bad after all. I wasn't about to tell Aunt

Sally about it ever, because she'd say no boy was supposed to see your bare shoulders till you were
engaged—something like that. I told Dad, though, and
he laughed. *Every*body laughed. Everybody but Pamela.

When I got to the bus stop the next morning,
Elizabeth said "Hi," but Pamela turned away.

"Pamela?" I said.

"Hi," she said coldly.

"What's wrong?"

"You should know," she said.

I stared at her back. "*How* should I know? I just got
up, ate my Cheerios, walked out here, and suddenly
you're mad at me."

"It's not this morning; it's yesterday," she said.

"What about yesterday?"

"The way you went around hogging attention. All
that Bubbles stuff."

"Pamela!" I said. "That's *my* fault? Who gave the
picture to Patrick in the first place?"

"I didn't know he was going to make a poster."

"Well, *I* didn't even know he had the picture! What
are you mad at *me* for?"

"Well, you certainly acted like you were enjoying
it," Pamela sniffed.

I was really getting angry with her. "So what do you
want me to do? Go rip it down?"

"Yeah, Pamela, it's not Alice's fault," Elizabeth said.
"She's just being a good sport about it."

Pamela stuck her hands in her pockets. "Well, if I
was you, I'd ask Patrick to take it down."

"If I was *you*, I wouldn't go around giving out pictures of friends unless I'd asked them, especially friends I'd promised to be loyal to for life," I said.

The bus came, Pamela and I took separate seats, and Elizabeth, not wanting to have to choose between us, sat at the back all by herself. The three girls who had promised to be friends forever were sitting three seats apart on the bus.

"Lester," I said after school. "I don't understand girls."

"Welcome to the club. You get any insights, share them with me. Who are you having problems with? Denise again?"

"Pamela." I pulled out the photos of the three of us in the bathtub and showed them to Lester.

"I've seen bare shoulders before," he said.

"That's not the *point*, Lester!" I told him, and explained about Pamela being jealous.

"That's all the problem?"

"Isn't it enough?"

"Simple as pie. You take *your* photo of *Pamela* down to the print store, get a poster-size copy made, and give it to some boy at school to put inside *his* locker. Boys will start calling *her* Bubbles, and then she'll be happy. I guarantee it."

"Do you really think this will work?"

"No, because then Elizabeth will feel left out, so if you want to avoid trouble, get a poster-size of each of them and let nature take its course."

"Okay, I will," I said, and two days later, with Pamela

still not speaking much to me, I arrived at school with two poster pictures rolled up in my school bag. I knew where Mark Stedmeister's locker was, so I went there first and waited for him even though he and Pamela were forbidden to date anymore because they kissed too much. He was really glad to get the picture, and put it on the inside of his locker door just the way Patrick had done with my picture.

The real problem was what to do with Elizabeth's poster. I finally gave it to a boy who always stares at Elizabeth in the cafeteria, and he just kept saying, "Wow! Wow!"

Bull's-eye! I said to myself.

By the end of the day, I was friends with Pamela again, but Elizabeth said she would never speak to me as long as she lived.

What happened with Pamela's poster was that Mark showed it to every boy who walked by, and they started calling her "Bubbles II." Whenever guys saw us walking together, they started singing that old song, "I'm Forever Blowing Bubbles."

What happened with Elizabeth's picture was that the jerk I gave it to didn't have the sense to put it on the door of his locker. He pinned it up on the bulletin board beside the trophy case, and someone came along and drew little red dots with Magic Marker where Elizabeth's breasts would be beneath the bubbles. Elizabeth almost fainted dead away when she found it, but that was after practically every boy in school had seen it.

I took the poster down and tore it up, but Elizabeth bawled all the way home on the bus.

"Elizabeth, I'm sorry," I told her. "I figured if I had one made of Pamela but not of you, *you'd* be mad."

"Did I *ask* you to do that?" she sobbed.

"No, but . . ."

"They put *dots* on mine, Alice!"

"Elizabeth, your picture wasn't any different from ours," Pamela tried to tell her. "Everybody knew the dots were just drawn there."

"But now everybody knows where my breasts are!" Elizabeth wailed.

"They knew where they were before!" I croaked. "Breasts don't migrate or anything."

"They'll think I'm *that* kind of g-girl."

"What kind is that?"

"Who lets people take pictures of her in bathtubs."

"But you are! I mean, you did!" I said, and she started bawling again.

I walked in our house, dumped my book bag on the floor, and bellowed, "I am resigning from the female species forever!"

"Welcome to the world of men," Lester said over his bag of pretzels.

I plopped myself down across from him. "Lester, if somebody gave you pictures of Marilyn and Crystal in the bathtub, what would you do with them?"

"Tape them on the ceiling over my bed," he said.

I gave him a look and went upstairs. But the worst

was yet to come. The phone rang, and it was Elizabeth's mother.

"Alice," she said sternly. "Would you come over, please? I'd like to talk with you."

I went back downstairs. "If I don't come home," I told him, "you can have everything in my room except my bracelet from Niagara Falls." And I marched across the street.

Mrs. Price met me at the door. Elizabeth was sitting in a corner of the living room, her eyes red, and she didn't even look up when I came in. I could tell that, mad as she was at me, she was still embarrassed that her mother had called me over.

"Please sit down, Alice," Mrs. Price said, and took a chair across from me. "I am very disappointed in you. Elizabeth gave you those pictures in confidence, and you had no right to make poster prints and give them out at school."

I tried to explain how Pamela had been mad at me and how I didn't want Elizabeth to feel left out.

Mrs. Price stared at me. "How could you possibly think Elizabeth would be angry if she didn't have a picture of herself in the bathtub pinned up on the school bulletin board?"

I knew that didn't sound right. "I don't know," I said miserably. "I guess I take stupid pills." I mean, what was there to say? Elizabeth was staring down at her lap, but I could tell she was trying not to smile when I said that.

Mrs. Price was quiet a moment. Then: "We have her reputation to think about, after all."

I nodded.

"So, Alice, if you'll promise that you'll never show that picture to anyone else, I won't object if you and Elizabeth remain friends."

I didn't tell her I'd already torn it up. "I promise not to show it to anyone else if Elizabeth will promise not to take any more pictures of me in the bathtub the next time I come here for a sleepover."

Mrs. Price looked horrified. "But ... it was just a girlish idea. . . . I mean, it wasn't for anyone else to see." She was flustered. "Surely, Alice, the other students don't think that this is the kind of thing we do when girls come to visit Elizabeth."

"Well," I said, "it never happened at anyone else's house."

Elizabeth had pressed her lips together, trying hard not to laugh, and watching Elizabeth made my own mouth start to stretch, and suddenly we couldn't hold back any longer.

Mrs. Price looked from me to Elizabeth and back again. Then she started laughing, too. "This is getting sillier by the minute," she said. "What do you say we forget the whole thing?"

"Agreed," I said.

"Agreed," said Elizabeth. She followed me out on the porch, and we laughed some more.

After dinner that night, I got a saucer of graham

crackers and stood in the doorway of the dining room where Dad was working on some papers at his table.

"Dad," I said, "how do you go your whole life without ever having anyone mad at you? I mean, how can you be a person that everybody likes?"

"You can't," said Dad, and went on writing.

"Well, how can I go for at least a year with everyone liking me?"

"Impossible."

I came over and sat down across from him.

"Toots," said Dad. Sometimes he calls me "Toots" when he wants to be really serious. "People who try to please everybody all the time turn out like oatmeal. You know that, don't you?"

"No."

"They become so bland, so boring, that no one can get very interested in them."

I wondered if that's what happened to Mr. Hensley.

"What you have to do first of all is be true to Alice McKinley. And if you're the *best* Alice you can be, you'll just naturally respect the right of other people to be *them*selves."

I ate another cracker and thought it over. "Is that something Mom would have said, or is that from you?"

"Consider that from both of us." Dad smiled.

I sighed. "I'm on good terms with Mr. Hensley again. I've made up with Pamela and Elizabeth, but I still don't know what to do about Denise Whitlock."

"I really can't tell you what to do, Al. I think that this one requires creative thinking."

"But I never *did* anything to her! She has no reason to hate me!"

"That's life, Al. Sometimes people hate other people for reasons they don't even understand themselves. But I trust you to think up something, and I have the feeling that when the time comes, you'll know what to do."

"To get even?"

"I didn't say that, did I?"

I kept wondering what Dad meant. All I could think of was how wonderful it would be to wait until Denise was in the shower in P.E., and then take not only her towel but her clothes as well and stuff them all in one of the toilets. I thought of the way she would look when she opened the shower curtain and discovered her towel was gone. How she'd have to walk naked out to the towel table to get another. How she'd come hulking back to her dressing cubicle, mad as blazes, to find that all her clothes were gone. How she'd beat me to a pulp. That wasn't the solution to anything, but I didn't have the foggiest idea what was.

12 ❀ *Taking Chances*

THINGS HAD been getting worse, not better, between Denise Whitlock and me. At first she hadn't seemed to like me because she didn't like all that snuffling and sneezing behind her in Language Arts. She disliked me even more when I got interviewed for the school newspaper. Then the three things happened she just couldn't forgive: Lester rescued me on Seventh Grade Sing Day just when she had center stage; I laughed when she fell on her stomach in P.E.; and boys started calling me Bubbles. Even though my hay fever was gone by December, the message was written all over her face—hers and her crowd's: *Get Alice.* It seemed as though they were just after me because I was there, because it had become habit.

They purposely bumped into me in the gym, tripped

me in the halls, flipped food at me in the cafeteria, laughed at every mistake, every flub, teased me about my hair, my clothes. If I ignored them, it didn't help. If I tried to laugh it off, it didn't help. If I was rude in return, it made things worse.

"I'd paste them one," said Pamela. "The next time you go by their table, drop an open carton of milk down Denise's fat neck."

"If it was me, I'd go to the principal," Elizabeth said. "I'd make him call Denise in and sit there while I told all the rotten things she'd done to me."

I was tempted, I'll admit. But I realized I had to make up my mind: Did I want to solve the problem or just get even?

I guess what I really wanted to do was get even first, *then* solve the problem, but the thing about getting even is you never do. When I sat down in my seat in Language Arts, though, and found that Denise had smeared Vaseline all over my desk top, I wanted in the worst way to clobber her, but how could I ever prove she'd done it?

"Al, what in the world did that pork chop ever do to you?" Les said at dinner. "You don't have to mutilate it." Dad was working late, and Lester and I had actually made a gourmet meal for just the two of us: pork chops and applesauce. "What's wrong?"

"Denise Whitlock."

"Denise Mack-Truck Whitlock?"

"That's the one." I told him all the things she'd done lately.

"It's time to get tough, Al. Cream her."

"You're kidding."

"Just haul off and let her have it."

"I'd get called to the principal's office."

"Go! Make a splash! Cause an uproar!"

I thought about it as I finished my meat. Would that be enough? I wondered. Even if I told the principal everything Denise had done to me and he punished her, too, even if her friends didn't pile up on me after school, she'd still go on hating my guts.

Lester went out later, so I decided to call Aunt Sally long distance. This was a big enough problem to see if she had any suggestions.

"Alice, dear, how are you?" she asked as soon as she heard my voice.

"Not so good," I answered. "Aunt Sally, what do you do when there's this girl who hates you?" And I told her a few things about Denise.

"Well, dear, it's difficult, I know, but I firmly believe that there's a soft spot in that girl, and if you can find it, you'll win her over."

I imagined probing Denise in the back during Language Arts, looking for her soft spot. I imagined Denise turning around and pasting me in the mouth.

"Here's what you do," said Aunt Sally. "You give a little Christmas party for some of your friends and invite Denise."

My stomach turned. "She wouldn't come," I said.

"Tell her there's a special present under your tree just for her. No girl can refuse a present."

"What if she still wouldn't come?"

"Tell her your big brother will be there and wants to meet her. Girls always like to meet their friends' brothers."

I almost choked. "They've already met," I said plaintively, and told her about Seventh Grade Sing Day.

"Oh, my, this *is* serious!" said Aunt Sally. "What you've got to do, then, is write her a letter and tell her how much you want to be her friend."

"But I *don't!*" I bleated. "I just want her to leave me alone."

"Write her a letter," Aunt Sally insisted, "and enclose a friendship ring. Tell her you bought it just for her."

I tried to imagine writing a letter like that to Denise. I imagined Denise going to school the next day and telling everyone that I had proposed. I imagined her wearing the ring in her ear. Her nose. Pinning my letter up on the bulletin board outside the cafeteria. I wondered if when my mom and Aunt Sally were girls, Aunt Sally had given Mom the same stupid advice she gave me. I wondered why I kept calling Aunt Sally in the first place.

I thanked her for her suggestion, said yes, we were all eating vegetables now and then, and no, Dad wasn't engaged or anything, and then I said good-bye and hung up. I decided that Dad had been right all along. This was a problem no one else could solve but me. I had to figure out how to deal with Denise all by myself.

When Dad came home later, he looked sort of down-in-the-mouth, sad and discouraged, and it occurred to me that Helen Lake had promised to visit him in November, and here it was December and she hadn't come. I couldn't believe I'd been so selfish that I hadn't even thought about Dad's problems. Only mine.

I heated up his dinner for him and then sat across the table while he ate.

"When's Helen Lake coming to visit, Dad?" I asked. Tactful, that's me.

"She isn't," he said. "I had a letter from her a few days ago."

I waited. Something *was* wrong, then. "She's not coming at all? Ever?"

Dad smiled just a little. "Well, 'ever' is a long time. Let's just say she's not coming any time soon."

"Oh," I said.

And when Dad realized I wasn't going to get up and walk away, he said, "It's like this, Al. Helen Lake and Janice Sherman have been friends for a long time— longer than I've known either one of them. And Helen realized that if I were to become serious about her, it would hurt their friendship. So she's opted to stay friends with Janice."

"You mean she chickened out," I said. "You mean she lost her chance to get married to the greatest man she'll ever meet."

"Hey, wait a minute! Who's talking marriage?" Dad grinned. "But I appreciate the compliment."

I wanted to make December really special for Dad after that and when Monday of the second week came around, I decided to concentrate only on Christmas.

Loretta Jenkins had holiday decorations up in the Gift Shoppe at the Melody Inn, we already had a light snow, I was getting along with all my teachers, and we were playing basketball in P.E. It was a time for gifts and music and evergreen and being nice to everybody. Mr. Hensley even wore a tie to class that day with microscopic bits of red in it.

I especially liked my Language Arts class because Miss Summers, with her blue-green eyes, made me forget about the fact that Denise was in it. Watching my teacher move about the front of the room, listening to her read in her velvety voice, I remembered how desperately I'd wanted to be in beautiful Miss Cole's room back in sixth grade, and how disappointed I was that I'd got Mrs. Plotkin instead. And now I wondered what Mrs. Plotkin was doing this Christmas and decided I'd send her a card. I was feeling kind toward the whole human race. That's what Christmas does for you, see. One thing leads to another. One minute I was listening to Miss Summers read *The Lady or the Tiger*, and the next I was thinking about my sixth-grade teacher.

Everybody, I guess, gets a little mellow around Christmas. Dad and Lester and I aren't real big on shopping, though. At Christmas we usually think of what we're going to do together instead of what we're going to give each other, so I wasn't surprised when Dad said that evening, "I've got three tickets for the *Messiah* Sing-Along. You two want to go?"

"Sure, why not?" said Lester.

"Al?"

"Yeah, I'll go," I said.

We've been going to *Messiah* Sing-Alongs as far back as I can remember, even in Chicago. If you're going to be one of the singers instead of the audience, you come early and practice a little. There's an orchestra and paid singers for the solo parts, but the public is invited to be part of the chorus.

Because Dad started taking me with him when I was small, I've always stood next to him, even though I don't sing. Dad's a tenor, and tenors stand next to altos, and he always manages to stand just at the edge of the tenors so I blend in with the women and don't look weird or anything. I think Dad lets me sit with the singers in hopes that all this music around me will cure my tone deafness, and of course it doesn't, but I like being in the middle of all that noise. I especially love it when everyone stands to sing the Hallelujah Chorus. I just hum through the other parts, and in the Hallelujah, everyone sings so loud that what I do doesn't matter. I sound just fine to me.

What I also like about December are the carols. Dad brings home new cassettes of Christmas music, so I can hear my favorite carols in a dozen different styles. "The Cherry Tree Carol" is one of my favorites—how Mary's engaged to Joseph, and she tells him she's pregnant by someone else. Wow! What a shocker! We've got two versions of that. In the first one, Mary asks Joseph to pick some cherries for her, but he gets mad and says the father of her baby can do it. Then the cherry tree bows low so Mary can pick them herself, and Joseph just stands around. In the second version, Joseph apologizes to Mary because he knows she's going to be the Mother of Jesus.

The next evening I'd just finished listening to the second version when Lester came home from the library.

"Lester," I said, "if you were engaged to Marilyn and she told you she was pregnant by someone else, what would you do?"

Lester hung up his jacket. "Is this a trick question?"

"Just checking," I told him.

The rest of the week was a week of taking chances, and it all happened in Miss Summers's classroom. We had already done folk tales, fables, and legends, and were finishing up a unit on the short story. Miss Summers mentioned that next semester we'd be reading biographies, autobiographies, and novels, and some of the class groaned.

She pushed her papers aside and came around to sit on the edge of her desk, the way she does when she has something important to say.

"I know that some of you think you don't like to read full-length books, but maybe, just maybe, you're in for a surprise," she said in her low voice. Her voice and her skin and her coral-colored sweater all seemed made out of the same soft stuff.

"I used to feel that way about music," she told us. "Classical music, I mean—music by Mozart and Brahms and Beethoven." She made a little face, and the tiny frown lines made pink creases in her forehead. "It just sounded like noise to me—all those violins and horns twanging and blaring at once. But I knew there must be something to it because so many people love it. I made up my mind that every day for a week, when I was preparing my dinner at night, I would play Mozart's Fortieth Symphony. It wouldn't be like an assignment. I didn't have to listen closely or anything. Just play the music. By the third evening I was beginning to hear melodies that were familiar. I realized I was listening for certain passages, and it was then I discovered just how full and rich and wonderful that kind of music can be. Every time I hear it again, there are surprises—things I hadn't caught before, and I'm always sorry when it's over."

She smiled at the class. "That's the way it is with books. *Good* books—full and rich and deep. And that's what I want you to discover. If you're in my class next semester, we're not going to worry so much about grammar. Don't even think about how you're going to sound when you read reports to the class. All I want you to do is enjoy. I want you to discover the *pleasure* of reading."

I was so glad I was scheduled for Miss Summers's class next semester I wanted to stand up and shout. For once in my life things were going my way.

And suddenly I wasn't thinking about books or school or Denise or even Christmas. I was thinking about Miss Summers cooking dinner all by herself, loving Mozart and Brahms and Beethoven, and when the bell rang at the end of class, I found my feet walking up to her desk, my face stretching into a smile, and my lips saying:

"Miss Summers, my dad and I wondered if you'd like to go with us to the *Messiah* Sing-Along on December twenty-second." I couldn't believe it myself.

Miss Summers looked at me with her blue-green eyes, sort of puzzled. "You and . . . your *father*, Alice?"

"Yes. He'd really like it if you could come. He's manager of the Melody Inn, and he likes Mozart, too."

"Over on Georgia Avenue? Why, that's where I buy my music!" she said.

I smiled even broader. "So could you come?"

"I sing alto and would be absolutely delighted," she said.

I grinned. "We'll let you know later about the time and everything."

"Thank you very much, Alice," she said. "I'll look forward to it."

"Me, too," I said.

I went out in the hall, leaned against the trophy case, and let out my breath.

What I had to do quick was get another ticket to the sing-along. As soon as I got home, I found the tickets on Dad's dresser and called the phone number on the envelope.

"I'm so sorry," the woman said, "but we're sold out. We sold out even earlier than last year."

"Even altos?" I asked.

"Especially altos," the woman told me.

I felt my heart slide right down to my toes. Then I had another idea. Since Dad had signed me up as an alto and I don't sing at all, Miss Summers could use my ticket and I could use Lester's. One nonsinging alto certainly equalled one nonsinging tenor.

When Lester came home later I said, "Les, do you *really* want to go to the *Messiah* Sing-Along?"

"Yeah," said Lester. "It sort of grabs me."

"Even if you got invited some place with Marilyn or Crystal?" I thought maybe I could work something out with one of them.

"Yeah, I'd still go to the sing-along because I know it means a lot to Dad," Lester said. "He's sort of lonely right now, you know."

I lay down on the rug and pretended I was dead. The only possible way out of the mess was to get sick the day of the sing-along and tell Dad that I'd invited Miss Summers to go in my place. Strep throat. Stomach flu. Appendicitis. I'd think of something.

What I thought of, actually, was that I hardly knew a thing about Miss Summers except that her eyes were blue-green and I liked her. Maybe she already had a boyfriend. Maybe he was a wrestler.

But that was only the first impulsive thing I did that week. When I got to Language Arts the next day, Denise not only jabbed me as I went to sharpen my pencil but left a pen mark on my jeans. I think if I had been in anyone's class but Miss Summers's, I might have hauled off and let her have it, like Lester said. But I didn't especially want to be sitting in the principal's office so close to Christmas, and I certainly didn't want to embarrass myself in front of my teacher.

Miss Summers, in a green knit dress, faced the class and said that we had just one more project to do before Christmas vacation.

"In preparation for the unit on biography next semester," she told us, "I want you to get some understanding of what's involved in writing about another person's life—what's important, what's not, and what circumstances and events help shape us. To give you some firsthand experience, I want each of you to do an interview of your own."

She walked over to the first person in the first row. "Beginning with you," she said, "every other person is an A. All the A's raise your hands, please."

We mentally counted off, and every other person raised his or her hand. I was an A.

"Hands down," said Miss Summers. "All the rest of you are B's. All the B's, hold up your hands."

The rest of the students put their hands in the air. Denise, I realized gratefully, was a B.

"I want you to interview each other," Miss Summers went on. "And to show I'm not entirely without mercy, I'll let you choose your own partners. Keep your hands in the air, B's, so we'll know who you are, and every A pick a B, starting with you," she said to the boy in front. "There's an even number in this class, so no one will be left out."

I wished there had been an uneven number in class

so that I could volunteer to write about Miss Summers herself, but that just wasn't in the picture.

"Ready?" she said.

The boy in the first row called out a friend's name across the room, and Miss Summers wrote it down in her notebook. I usually hate things like this because it's embarrassing to the person who's chosen last. But this time I knew for a fact that Denise Whitlock would be chosen last—none of her crowd was in our room. She knew it, too. I could tell by the way her shoulders slumped, and I was delighted.

I was sitting in the last seat in the second row, and as the A's in front of me began choosing B's as partners, I looked around to see whom I would pick. And suddenly I remembered what Dad had said about how, when the time came, I would know what to do.

"Sue Cranston," said the A two seats in front of me.

The teacher looked at me. "Alice?"

"Denise Whitlock," I told her, heart pounding.

13 ❀ *Questions and Answers*

DENISE SAT like a chunk of concrete. Her hand dropped like a signal flag as soon as I said her name, and now there was nothing moving at all. I wasn't even sure she was breathing.

When all the class had been paired up, Miss Summers explained the assignment: "I want the A's to interview the B's first, then vice versa, using the charts we made last September as an outline. You may have the last couple of minutes of class today to plan when you can get together with your partner. But for the next twenty minutes or so, let's talk about the things that influence us and make us the type of people we are, whether we're the common, ordinary variety or one of the famous you'll be reading about next semester. Family size, values, religion, scholastic record, hobbies, parents' occupations . . ." Miss Summers started writing these things on the blackboard while we copied them in our notebooks.

Denise wasn't writing anything at all. I didn't see her shoulders or elbows move once. She hates my guts, I thought.

Miss Summers glanced at the clock finally. "Oh, dear, I've talked too long. You've got about thirty seconds, class, to talk to your partners. See what you can work out."

Kids started calling across the room to each other, moving about. Denise gathered up her stuff.

"Denise?" I said. "When do you want to meet?"

She only half turned. "Drop dead," she said over her shoulder.

"Remember, people, these are due the day before Christmas vacation, and they count fifty percent of your six weeks' grade," Miss Summers said.

Denise stopped and stared at the wall. Elizabeth told me once that she'd heard that if Denise failed any more subjects, she'd be so far behind she probably wouldn't be able to go on to high school when the time came.

"After lunch tomorrow in the library," Denise muttered finally, not even looking at me, and stalked from the room.

I felt weird the rest of the day—sort of high and nervous, like I'd drunk twelve cups of coffee. My heart was racing.

As soon as I got on the bus, I told Pamela and Elizabeth what I'd done.

"You *didn't*!" Pamela said.

"I did."

"Alice, of all the people you could have picked . . . !"

"I know. That's why I did it."

"Boy, Alice, you've got nerve!" said Elizabeth. "Can't you just *imagine* what she'll write about you?"

I shrugged. "She has to turn it in, remember."

I told Dad and Lester at dinner. Dad paused, with the bowl of spaghetti in his hand, eyebrows raised high, and beamed at me. "Good *thinking*, Al!" he said.

"Not bad," Les agreed. "Now you're the one calling the shots."

It wasn't as though I had thought of it myself, though. If the chance hadn't dropped in my lap, I'd probably still be on square one. But Dad says that half the time you've got to make your own opportunities and the other half you have to be able to see the ones that are already there.

I felt so great when I went up to my room later, with Christmas music drifting up from the stereo, that I forgot all about my other problem. Then I happened to look at my calendar and saw the *Messiah* date circled. I sank down on the bed and stared at it.

Part of me wanted to go downstairs, while Dad and Lester were in such a good mood, tell them what I'd done, and ask Dad if he'd mind taking Miss Summers to the sing-along instead of me. Then I thought how I would ruin his digestion and his evening as well, and I had no right to do that. I'd had no right to invite Miss Summers in the first place, of course. They were Dad's tickets, he'd chosen to take Lester and me, and if he'd wanted to take a woman instead, he would have. What he was looking forward to was quality time with his son and daughter. What he was going to get was an afternoon with Lester and a woman he didn't even know.

And that was only half of it. When Dad went to pick her up, Miss Summers would find herself in the company of two strange men. The girl who had invited her wouldn't even be there. Maybe she wouldn't get in the car. Maybe she'd phone the police.

I wasn't about to call Aunt Sally on this one. I'd got myself into it, and the only way out that I could see was to wait until the day of the sing-along, then tell Dad I wasn't feeling too well, go upstairs and call Miss Summers on the extension phone, tell her how my brother was going to use my ticket instead of me, then go down and tell Dad I was too sick to go and had invited my Language Arts teacher in my place.

The next day in class, Denise didn't even look at me. I wasn't there as far as Denise Whitlock was concerned. Her friends were pretty quiet, too. Once or twice they glanced in my direction in P. E. but didn't say anything. It was okay by me.

The same thing happened in the cafeteria. They sat in the same place, a few tables away, but Denise sort of turned her back to me. I finished first and went on over to the library to wait.

Our library is divided into two big rooms—one where you have to be really quiet, and the other half, the open section, where you can do homework to-gether. I found a table along the wall and put my books on it, then got out my pen and notebook and waited.

I didn't think she was going to come. It would be just like her, too, to leave me sitting there, waiting. Lunch period is over at 12:45, and she didn't come until almost 12:30. She yanked out the chair across from me, slammed her books on the table, and sat down with a thud.

"Hi," I said. She only sneered. "You want me to ask questions, or you just talk, or what?" I asked.

"This wasn't my idea," she said. "Shoot."

"Okay," I said, trying to keep my voice civil. "We're supposed to exchange those family tree charts we made in September." I handed her mine. She stuffed it in her notebook. "Mine's lost," she said.

I really had to struggle to keep my temper. "Well, I'll just start with basic questions, then," I told her. "Where you were born, how many brothers and sisters, where your parents work, stuff like that."

She tossed a pencil onto the table. "Detroit, Michigan; four brothers and a sister; Mom works for a dry-cleaning plant, and my dad runs a bowling alley."

It was like pulling weeds to get anything more out of Denise. She told me only what I asked, nothing else. We could have got twice as much done if she'd only cooperated a little, but she wasn't about to give an inch.

"We've got lots more to do," I said, when the bell rang. "Meet here Monday?"

"I guess." She picked up her stuff and pushed her way through the chairs and tables to the door.

Bingo! I said to myself.

On Monday in Language Arts, Miss Summers looked more beautiful than ever, and I wondered if I was only imagining it. She talked about how, from studying the lives of others, we learn about ourselves and our own place in the world. "But no matter how truthful a biographer sets out to be," she said, "his writing is influenced to some degree by how he feels about his subject."

Then she talked about John Gunther's book, *Death Be Not Proud*, a biography of his son who died of cancer at seventeen, and how the relationship between author and subject could be as close as father/son, or as distant as Carl Sandburg writing about Abraham Lincoln. Not only did her eyes shine as she talked about books she loved, but her voice sounded like music. I wondered if her eyes would shine like that when she talked to Dad about Mozart. *If* she talked to Dad about Mozart. If the afternoon even came off at all.

I imagined Lester and Dad and Miss Summers all sitting like fence posts at the concert, none of them speaking, and everyone hating me down to my toenails.

That noon Denise was at the library five minutes earlier. She didn't look any friendlier than she had before, but I think she realized that we had only five more days to get our interviews done, so we'd better get on with it.

This time she looked over at the list I'd copied from

the board. "What else do we have to cover?" she asked. "I have to interview you yet, you know."

"I know," I said. "We'll have to hustle." I read some more of the list: "Health problems, places you've lived, death of a family member, pets. . . . She also said we can skip anything we like or add something that isn't on the list."

"Gee, thanks." Denise snorted.

I waited. Denise waited. This time, though, she wasn't talking to the wall the way she had before. Her eyes were on me.

"How come?" she said.

I studied her. Her eyes were green, like mine. I could have told you every freckle on the back of her neck or arms, but I couldn't have told you the color of her eyes.

"How come what?"

"You know. How come you chose me?"

I almost said something smart, like, "Well, I had to choose someone," or "You were in my line of vision." Instead, I just said, "Because I wanted to."

She frowned. "Just getting even, huh?"

I shrugged. "Just getting to know you, that's all."

She gave a little smile, the first time Denise Whitlock ever smiled at me when it didn't seem to mean *I'll get you later*, and then she said, "Denise Whitlock, age fourteen; hobbies: teasing; problems: teasing; parents' values: I don't know, I never asked."

Every day went a little better than the day before with Denise. By Friday we forgot about the questionnaire and just started talking, telling our own stories in our own words. I'd thought that when it was her turn to do the interviewing, she'd really sock it to me, but Denise was surprisingly gentle.

"Problems?" I said when she asked. And then I smiled a little: "Denise Whitlock."

I was really surprised to see her blush. She didn't look at me. Her hand paused above the paper, like, what was she supposed to do now?

So I went right on: "Another of my problems is that I can't carry a tune. I never could. I just can't sing. Everyone else in my family can except me."

Denise looked at me curiously. "What happens? I mean, if you try?"

"It never comes out the right note. And the worst part is that I can't tell the difference. It usually sounds okay to me. Can you sing?"

"I thought everybody could."

"Well, everybody can't."

Denise wrote it down. "I guess we've all got something," she said.

"Something?"

She gave a half smile. "The way I look, the way you sing."

"I guess so," I said.

The interviews were almost over, and she hadn't asked me any questions I really minded. But there was one, I discovered, that I couldn't answer.

"I don't remember too much about my mother," I was telling her. "She died when I was five, and I think

Aunt Sally took over for a while, helping raise me. Sometimes I confuse memories of Aunt Sally with Mom, and that really freaks my dad out."

"What did she die of?" Denise asked.

"She was sick, I think. I mean, it wasn't an accident or anything." I stared at the pencil in Denise's hand. "I don't even know what it was. That's weird, isn't it? I don't think I ever asked."

That night Dad and I were scrubbing the bathroom together. We'd been putting if off for about three weeks, and the floor was getting so dirty that when you stepped out of the tub in your bare feet, you had to wipe them again to get all the hair and lint and dirt off them.

Scrubbing the bathtub hurts Dad's back, so we have this system: I do the tub and he does everything else. I always scrub the bathtub in my bathing suit. I get in with a rag and a can of Ajax, and while Dad scrubs the sink and toilet, I scrub down the sides of the bathtub with cleanser. Then I turn on the shower and sort of skate around the tub barefoot, rubbing off the bottom and sides with my feet.

I was in the Ajax stage and Dad was working on the sink when I said, "Dad, was Mom sick a long time before she died?"

I never seem to give Dad much warning when I ask things like that. He paused, studying his own reflection in the mirror, and then he went on polishing the faucets: "It was about four months, Al."

"That must have been pretty rough on you."

"It was rough on all of us, honey. Maybe you don't remember much, but you were pretty confused at the time. Lester took it awfully hard. He cried a lot. We all did."

I stood up in my bathing suit, Ajax running down my leg. "What did she die of?"

Dad glanced over at me. "We never told you that? It was leukemia. Once we discovered what her symptoms meant, she went fast."

I don't know what it was—the sight of Dad's face in the mirror or the words, "She went fast," but suddenly I felt the tears.

"Dad . . ." I gulped.

And then he was standing beside the bathtub with his arms around me, patting my back, and we both cried a little. When it was over, I turned on the shower and let the water rinse the tub and my face at the same time.

When I was clean and dry, I went to my room to start writing the biography of Denise Whitlock, and then I remembered that the *Messiah* Sing-Along was Sunday afternoon and I hadn't said one word to Miss Summers about when we'd pick her up. The tickets had said "Singers, 3:00. Audience, 4:00." I looked up "Summers" in the phone book, then realized I didn't even know her first name. I panicked. I hadn't told Miss Summers what time we'd pick her up; I didn't know her first name; I didn't know where she lived; and Dad didn't know her at all.

Stay calm, I told myself. What would Mom do if she

was here? That didn't help. If Mom was here, we
wouldn't be taking my Language Arts teacher to the
concert.

I counted the number of "Summers" in the Maryland
directory. There were sixty-four, and seventeen of
them were women. The others had either men's names
or initials. I looked for any female Summers that lived
in Silver Spring. There were four. I called them. Three
answered and said they were not my teacher. The
fourth wasn't home.

Okay, I told myself, there are only three things that
could happen, and it's not the end of the world: You
will somehow, miraculously, find out the phone number of Miss Summers; she will find our phone number
and call us; no one will call anybody and you will flunk
Language Arts.

I put in my three hours at the Melody Inn the next
morning. Janice Sherman seemed to be adjusting to
the fact that Dad couldn't allow himself to love her,
because she had a little sprig of holly pinned to her
blouse, and she smiled and said good morning like she
really meant it.

I went about my work dusting all the pianos, and
suddenly I remembered that Miss Summers had said
that this was where she bought her music. I didn't know
what kind of music, but if she had an account with us,
I might be able to find her address. I walked back to
the office and looked up "Summers" in the records.
And this is when the Great December Miracle happened. There was an account for Sylvia Summers, in

Kensington, for two different orders of piano music—one, a year and a half ago, and the other in September. I copied down the address and phone number, and as soon as I got home at noon, dialed her number.

A low voice said: "Hello. This is Sylvia Summers. I'm not at home right now, but if you will leave your name and number, I'll call back as soon as possible. Please wait for the beep."

The beep was in my heart, because that was my teacher's voice, all right, even though it was coming through a machine.

Beep, went the machine.

"Uh ... Sylvia ... I mean, Miss Summers ... this is Alice McKinley, and we'll pick you up at—well, *some*body will pick you up at two o'clock tomorrow for the *Messiah* Sing-Along. We're really happy you can go. Good-bye."

Then I dropped the receiver like it was hot or something, and wondered why I'd said two o'clock. Kensington wasn't far from the church on Cedar Lane where the sing-along would be.

What were we supposed to talk about all that time in between? Then I remembered I didn't have to worry about that because I wouldn't be there. Maybe Dad and Lester could take her for ice cream first or something.

I went in the bathroom and stood at the mirror to work on my "sick" face. I wrinkled up my forehead a little and let the corners of my mouth sag. I didn't look very sick to me. I took a wash cloth and rubbed my face all over as hard as I could. One minute. Two minutes. I looked in the mirror. My face was fiery red.

At dinner that night, I picked at my food and finally said I was going upstairs to lie down.

"You sick, Al?" Dad asked.

"Sort of," I murmured.

"We've got tickets for the *Messiah* tomorrow," he said.

"Yeah. Well, maybe I'll feel better by then," I told him.

"They cost seven dollars each," Dad said, to make me well in a hurry.

"Don't worry," I heard Lester tell him as I started upstairs. "If she can't go, I'll invite Crystal."

14 ✿ Hallelujah

I DIDN'T get out of bed Sunday morning. My stomach growled, and I wished I'd at least smuggled some Ritz crackers upstairs to eat until Dad came to see what was wrong.

Ten o'clock came. Eleven. Eleven forty-five. I couldn't stand it any longer. I put on my socks and padded down to the kitchen. Dad and Lester were in the living room reading the paper and didn't even look up when I passed by in the hall. Just for that, I ate the last three slices of cinnamon bread and the next-to-the-last banana.

I was finishing up all the orange juice, too, when Dad came out in the kitchen. "How you feeling?" he asked.

"Sort of wobbly," I said, trying to hide the banana peel.

"Think you can go this afternoon?"

"I hope so. I'm not sure."

The phone rang, and my stomach flip-flopped. What if it was Miss Summers saying she couldn't go, and Dad would say, "*Who* can't go *where*?"

It was Crystal Harkins calling Lester. Dad was just pouring himself some more coffee when Lester put down the phone in the hallway and came out in the kitchen.

"Dad, Crystal has two tickets to the *Messiah* and wants me to go with her. I—"

Dad wheeled around in exasperation. "What am I going to do? Go to this thing all by myself? I've got three tickets, but you're going with Crystal and Al's sick. I thought we might do something as a family for a change."

"Relax! Re*lax*!" said Lester. "I'll still sit with you. Okay?"

"But I'll have two extra tickets," Dad said.

I leaped up. "No, you won't. I'm feeling fine, really. I'm going!"

Dad turned around and stared at me.

"And I'll get someone to go with us. Okay?"

"Well, okay." Dad shrugged. "Tell Pamela or Elizabeth we're leaving at two-thirty sharp."

I sank down in my chair again, relief all over my face, legs spread out under the table.

"That was a fast recovery," said Dad.

"I guess it was the orange juice," I told him. I could feel his eyes on me as I went upstairs to get dressed.

I took a shower, washed my hair, rubbed some of Lester's deodorant under my arms, and topped it off with a little talcum powder Aunt Sally had sent for my birthday. I smelled like peach ice cream. Then I went through my closet twice looking for something to wear, and finally took out a black velvet skirt that came down below my knees and used to be my cousin Carol's, and a pink blouse that came from I don't know where. Sears, probably.

It took three tries to get my panty hose on right so that they didn't feel as if they were twisted around one leg. I put on my black flats, and stuck a pink barette in my hair. Then I went downstairs. Dad whistled.

"Is that my daughter?" he said. "I didn't realize this was a dress-up occasion. I was just going to wear my cords and a turtleneck."

"Why don't you wear a tie?" I suggested.

Dad was studying me. "I'll wear a coat and tie if you'll change your blouse."

I looked down. "What's wrong with it?"

"It just doesn't seem to go with that skirt somehow."

"But why? I have to know *why* things don't go with things."

"Well, sweetheart, I wish I could tell you, but—Les, come here a minute, will you?"

Lester lumbered in from the other room and grabbed some grapes off the counter.

"She look okay to you? Her clothes?" Dad asked.

"Nix the blouse," said Lester.

"Why?" I could feel tears in my eyes. I didn't care about the blouse, I just had to know what was wrong. If I had a mother, she would know. Did I have to call Aunt Sally long distance every time I tried to dress up? Why did I have to be raised by two men who only knew about football and music and oil changes?

"Tell you what, let me look through your closet and see if I can find something better," Dad said. I followed him upstairs and plopped sullenly down on my bed while he looked.

"This one," he said, pulling out a white satin-looking blouse that also used to be Carol's. "It's heavier material, Al, so it goes better with a heavy velvet skirt. It also has long sleeves. That short-sleeved pink thing was made to be worn with thin summer skirts. *That's* why. Okay?"

"Well, why didn't you say so in the first place? How am I supposed to get through junior high and high school if you never know what's wrong?"

"Be patient with me, Al. I'm doing the best I can."

And then I felt awful. I grabbed his arm and squeezed it. "Okay," I said.

I felt I couldn't go another minute without telling him about Miss Summers. "Dad," I called, when he was halfway down the hall.

He turned.

"We've got to pick someone up at two."

"Two? It takes only fifteen minutes to get to Cedar Lane."

"Well, I goofed, I guess, and told her two."

"Call her back and tell her two-thirty."

"I—I can't. We've got to pick her up, and I already said two."

Dad's shoulders slumped and he thrust his hands in his pockets. "Al, you are driving me two hundred per-cent nuts."

"I'm sorry," I said.

"Who's going? Pamela or Elizabeth? Just call and—"

"Neither one. Someone from school."

"Where does she live?"

I gave him the address on Saul Road. He sighed in exasperation and went into his bedroom to dress.

All the way over to Kensington in the car, I knew I should tell him what to expect, but I lost my nerve.

"What's her name?" Dad said, as he fiddled with the car radio. "It's a her, isn't it?"

I nodded. "Sylvia."

"New friend?"

"Sort of."

"What class is she in?"

"Language Arts."

"Well, it's nice to see you making new friends, Al. Branching out a little."

When we got to Saul Road, Dad leaned forward, checking house numbers, then brought the car to a stop outside a tiny little house, and kept the motor idling. "Run up and get her," he said. "I don't like to honk."

"Dad, I think maybe you'd better go to the door."

Dad leaned back and closed his eyes. "*Three* hundred percent nuts! Al, will you *please* go get your girlfriend and quit this quibbling?"

I stared down at my hands. "She's not a girlfriend. She's my teacher."

Dad's foot fell off the pedal in shock. The car jerked forward and the engine died. He stared at me a moment wordlessly. "Say that again," he said, and he wasn't smiling.

"I invited my Language Arts teacher," I said softly. "She said she loved Mozart, and I just thought she might like to come because she's so nice."

"How long ago did you invite her, Al? Just this morning? Without asking me?"

I swallowed. "Last week."

"We didn't have an extra *ticket* last week!"

"I know. I was going to be sick and stay home."

"*Four hundred* percent nuts!" said Dad, and bolted back in his seat. "Does that woman need help getting up and down stairs, Al? How old is she?"

"I—I don't know."

"Alice McKinley, you are the *limit*!" said Dad, unbuckling his seat belt and getting out of the car. He slammed the door and went up the walk like he was out to kill a dragon, but slowed down a little as he started up the steps. I saw him rub his neck, then ring the doorbell.

For a while I thought Miss Summers wasn't home. Maybe she forgot all about it and had gone out of town for the weekend, leaving her answering machine on.

Maybe she'd never listened to her messages, and decided I hadn't really meant my invitation after all.

Then I saw the glass door move. It opened, and there was Miss Summers, stepping out onto the porch in a bright blue coat and high heels.

I think Dad was in shock. He sort of backed up, then stepped forward again, ran his hand through his hair, then shook the hand Miss Summers was holding out to him. His face was the color of a shrimp cocktail, and he stared straight ahead as they came back down the walk, Miss Summers chattering away.

As I watched, I tried to figure out just how old she was. Older than Lester, I was sure of that. Older than my cousin Carol, but younger than Aunt Sally. Younger than Elizabeth's mother, but not Pamela's. Maybe about as old as Pamela's mother. Thirty? Thirty-five?

I smiled as she came over to the car, and she was smiling, too.

Dad opened my door. "Al, why don't you hop in the backseat and let Miss Summers sit in front?" he said.

But Miss Summers already had the back door open. "Oh, no, this will be fine," she said, getting in. "How are you, Alice? How nice of you to invite me."

I grinned back. "I like your coat," I said.

"So do I," she purred. "The warmest, softest thing . . ."

Dad got in, but he didn't even look at me.

"I've been to only one *Messiah* Sing-Along, but that was years ago, and I always wanted to go again," my teacher said. "So here I am."

"Here we are!" I chirped happily.

Dad turned the key in the ignition and swallowed. "My daughter asked you to be ready rather early, I'm afraid. We'll probably be among the first ones there."

"That's fine. I can believe that of Alice because she's never late to class, either."

"That's good to hear," said Dad. I beamed at Dad, but he still wouldn't look at me. "I hope her school work is as good as her punctuality," he added.

"Good and getting better," said my teacher.

I beamed again. I felt like the Cheshire cat. And then it happened.

"You have a wonderful store," Miss Summers said.

Dad looked surprised. I saw him glance at her in his rearview mirror. "The Melody Inn?"

There was a pause. "Of course."

"So you've been in it, then! Yes, it *is* a good store. I'm so glad you like it."

There was no other sound from the backseat, and I knew I'd goofed by not telling Dad earlier. Miss Summers had believed me when I'd said that Dad and I were inviting her. She probably figured Dad had seen her in the store, found out more about her, and then suggested we invite her to go with us. Now she knew that the invitation was only from me.

I closed my eyes. Nobody spoke much again all the way to the church. Dad couldn't figure out what was wrong, but he knew something was bothering Miss Summers. I knew they were going to hate each other.

I knew they were going to hate me. This was going to be a terrible afternoon, and Miss Summers would want to be taken home as soon as possible after the concert was over.

We all climbed out in the parking lot, and no one was smiling. I couldn't stand it any longer and flattened myself against the side of the car.

"It's my fault!" I cried. "Miss Summers, I invited you because you said you liked Mozart, and then I realized we didn't have an extra ticket and tried, but they were all sold out, and I was going to be sick at the last minute so you could use mine, but Lester's going with his girlfriend. Please don't be angry. I just wanted you to come, and I think Dad's glad you're here even though he didn't know it."

Dad looked more like a cooked lobster this time than a shrimp. His face was almost as red as his tie. Suddenly Miss Summers threw back her head and laughed. She put one arm around me and laughed some more. Then Dad started to smile, little chuckles coming from his throat, and finally we were all smiling.

"Alice," my teacher said, "this is exactly the kind of thing I would have done when I was your age." She looked at Dad. "I wondered why you looked so surprised when I answered the door. You probably thought I was going to be a young friend of your daughter's."

"No, he thought you were going to be an old lady," I said.

Now Dad was laughing, and he grabbed an arm of

each of us and started for the building. "The important thing, Miss Summers, is that you're here," he said.

"Please call me Sylvia, Ben."

"Sylvia," he said, and we went inside.

It was easy after that. Now that things were out in the open, nobody had to pretend. We laughed again when we got inside and saw that no one was there yet but the orchestra. I wanted to take seats in the very first row of the singers' section, but Dad decided that was a little too close, so we got third row instead, right in the middle, about where the tenors and altos would meet. Dad went in first to save a seat for Lester, my teacher followed him, then I came last to save a seat for Crystal. That's just how I wanted it. I was still afraid to sit too close to Dad.

By 2:45, the singers' section began filling up fast. When Lester and Crystal came in, I waved.

"Excuse me . . . excuse me . . . ," Crystal kept saying as she made her way into our row from the other end, Lester behind her. "Merry Christmas, Alice." She smiled when she sat down on the other side of me, meaning she was delighted that she, not Marilyn, had Lester for the day, and maybe we'd be sisters-in-law after all.

"Merry Christmas," I told her. What I didn't tell her was that Lester was spending Christmas Eve with Marilyn. He'd already told me.

Lester sat down on the other side of Dad, then leaned forward to see if Crystal was settled in okay, and suddenly his lips fell apart and he positively stared.

"Miss Summers, this is my son, Lester, and his friend Crystal Harkins," said Dad.

Lester and Miss Summers shook hands across Dad's lap, Lester still gawking at my teacher.

When everybody had settled in and Dad and Miss Summers were talking again, I heard somebody go "Pssst!" and looked around behind my teacher. Lester was leaning way back in his chair.

"Who *is* she?" he mouthed.

I smiled sweetly. "Sylvia," I whispered, and faced forward again, folding my hands on my purse.

As last-minute singers took their seats, I could catch little snatches of conversation between Dad and my teacher:

". . . when Alice was five."

"Oh, I'm so sorry . . ."

". . . doing okay. I think we'll make it. How about you? You teach, but you're a musician, too?"

". . . the piano. I love your selection of sheet music."

I happily wiggled my toes.

The soloists arrived, and the rehearsal began. After we'd got the basic instructions and practiced a few numbers, the ushers opened the doors, and the audience filed in.

The *Messiah* is really long, and you have to sit through lots of solos, but some of them are good. I liked to sit there listening to the story of Jesus in song and sort of pretending I was Mary, just finding out from the angel that I'm pregnant, only I get it mixed up with "The Cherry Tree Carol." I kept waiting for the song about Mary asking Joseph to gather her some cherries, and then remembered Handel didn't write it.

Near the end, when everybody stood up to sing the Hallelujah Chorus, I sang, "*Hal*–le–lu–jah! *Hal*–le–lu–jah!" right along with them, and if Crystal or Miss Summers realized I was off-key, they didn't let on.

When it was all over, we stood there talking while the musicians packed up their instruments. Dad explained to Lester and Crystal that Miss Summers was my Language Arts teacher, and Lester looked back and forth from Miss Summers to me. I just smiled sweetly again and glanced away, and then my breath almost stopped because there, among the sopranos next to the wall, was Marilyn. She was with a girlfriend, but her eyes were on Lester and Crystal, who hadn't seen her.

I didn't tell Lester that he probably wouldn't be spending Christmas Eve with Marilyn after all. I figured he was a big boy and could take care of himself.

Lester and Crystal went somewhere in Lester's car, but I was so afraid Dad would take Miss Summers right home that I invited her to our house.

"I can make grilled cheese sandwiches, and there's butter pecan in the freezer," I told Dad. And when he still looked horrified, I added, "The bathroom's clean, remember."

Miss Summers started laughing again, and so did Dad, but that's what we did. Came to our house. I rushed upstairs and put a fresh towel in the bathroom for Miss Summers, because I saw Aunt Sally do that once when we came to visit unexpectedly. Then I set to work on the sandwiches while Dad played the piano for Sylvia.

He liked her, I could tell. She asked for a certain piece by Brahms that's one of Dad's favorites, and he smiled as he began to play it. She hummed. I pretended not to watch, but every time I passed the door of the kitchen, I looked. Dad was still smiling, and Miss Summers was still humming.

We ate at the coffee table in the living room, and Miss Summers took off her shoes so she could sit more easily on the floor. Her toenails were polished.

"You have pretty toes," I said.

"Thank you," she told me, and ate a carrot stick. I served carrot sticks, cheese sandwiches, applesauce, and butter pecan ice cream (which I hate, but I took all the nuts out of mine first).

"This has been a really lovely afternoon," Miss Summers said at last, "but I've got to get home. I tell you what. Why don't we drive through the grounds of the Mormon temple on the way back and see all their lights. Did you know that at Christmas they put thousands and thousands of tiny white lights on the trees on their property?"

Dad and I didn't know that, so we drove to Kensington and I let Miss Summers sit up front with Dad. There was already a long line of cars at the gate, and we oohed and aahed at the thousands of little sparkles there in the darkness as Dad drove us around.

I could tell that he was having a good time because

he didn't seem to be in any hurry to take Miss Summers home—drove right by the exit to go around again. When we finally got to Miss Summers's house, though, I wished I wasn't along. I wished that she'd invite Dad in, and they'd talk and talk and some day I'd have a new mother.

She said good-night to me, and told me again what a nice time she'd had. Then Dad walked her up to the door. They didn't kiss or hold hands or anything. Just talked some more. Finally she went inside and Dad came back and got in the car. I was still in the back-seat.

"Get up front, Al," he said.

Uh oh, I thought. I got out the back and climbed in the front. "Don't the Mormons have nice lights?" I said.

"Al ..."

"I *really* liked the concert, Dad."

"Al!"

I shut up.

Dad started the engine, and when the car was moving down the block, he said, "Don't you ever do that again."

My heart sank. "I—I thought we all had a good time."

"You thought I would fall in love and marry your teacher and you'd have a mother, that's what you thought. Well, things don't work that way, Al."

"But you had a nice time!"

"I did."

"And so did she! I *know* it!"

"She seemed to."

"Well, then, what's the—?"

"You don't know the first thing about love, Al. And she's too young for me."

"How young is she?"

"I don't know."

"You *liked* her!" I insisted.

"Yes, I did, but I have no idea how she feels about me. Not really. For all I know, she's dating other men and may even be serious about one of them."

"Then why did she come out with us?"

"Because you asked her."

"Because she thought *you* asked her, too!" I corrected.

"Listen, Al. I asked what she was doing Christmas Eve, if she'd like to go out to dinner with me, and she said she was spending the holidays with a friend."

There was still hope. "Maybe it's a girlfriend."

"I think she would have mentioned that if it was. And I don't want you doing anything, *any*thing, to get us together again. If we see each other some more, that's up to us, not you. Is that strictly understood?"

"Yes," I said in a voice I could hardly hear.

"No hints, no suggestions, no nothing. I *mean* it! This woman or any other."

"Okay," I said softly.

We drove almost all the way home in silence, but a few blocks from our house, I realized that Dad was whistling softly under his breath: *Hallelujah! Hallelujah!*

"Hal–le–e–e–lu–jah!" I bellowed out loud. Off-key, of course.

That made Dad laugh, and we sang it the rest of the way home. The Hallelujah Chorus. The only thing missing was the orchestra, and of course we couldn't stand up to sing.

On Monday, the last day before Christmas vacation, Denise and I both turned in our biographies. We let each other read them first, which was one of the rules, so we could change anything we didn't like or thought was too personal. But neither of us did.

Mine was longer and neater than hers, but hers was better than I'd thought it would be. One of the things we were supposed to do in the write-up was analyze what obstacles we thought the other person had to overcome to be a success, and what she had going for her.

I wrote that Denise had to overcome her habit of bullying other people if she wanted to make new friends, and that what she had going for her was that she was a leader; she could persuade other people to do what she wanted. I think she was surprised I'd called her a leader.

Denise, in turn, wrote that I was too sensitive about not being able to carry a tune, and she said what I had going for me was guts. That's just the way she put it. That I took chances. I sort of liked that, too.

Just as I was going out the door to get the bus, Denise passed me in the hall.

"Merry Christmas, Denise," I yelled.

"You, too," she said.

When I sat down with Pamela and Elizabeth, Pamela said, "I can't believe it. I just can't. I never thought you and Denise would be friends as long as you lived."

"Neither did I," I told her. "Life's weird, isn't it?"

"After all she did to you!" said Elizabeth. "I'm not sure I could ever make up with her until she apologized."

"Maybe she did," I said, "in her own way."

Two things happened the day before Christmas. I found a note in our mailbox from Miss Summers, thanking me for inviting her to the concert. "Please tell your father that it was a wonderful afternoon," she wrote, "and I hope we can do something like that again soon." I yelped with delight when I read it, and showed it to Dad. He didn't say anything, probably because his smile was so wide.

The other thing that happened, though, was that Marilyn called and told Les that she had other plans for Christmas Eve.

"Lester," I said, "I don't understand. If Marilyn doesn't want to get engaged, why is she mad that you're going out with Crystal?"

"Marilyn doesn't want a ring yet," Lester explained, "but she wants to be 'engaged to be engaged.' Crystal would marry me tomorrow, but I don't think I want a girl who's all that eager."

I didn't understand any more than I did before. Lester, though, wasn't as upset as I thought he'd be.

"I don't know," he told Dad. "Maybe I'll just 'batch'

it and not go out with either one of them for a while. It'll be good to hang out with the guys for a change. Women are too complicated."

"Sometimes," said Dad.

About six o'clock, our relatives in Tennessee called to see how all us folks in "Silver Sprangs" were doing. Then we called Aunt Sally to wish her and Uncle Milt and Carol a merry Christmas, and then we realized we didn't have anything good to eat in the house.

"Want to go out for dinner?" Dad asked us. "Your choice."

"Let's eat Mexican," Les said.

The restaurant's only a few blocks away, so we decided to walk it. We put on our coats and found snow flurries in the air again when we got outside. Not snow, just flurries. That's mostly the way it is in Maryland.

It was cold enough to see our breath, though, and I grabbed hold of Dad's arm on one side and Lester's on the other, and sort of hopped to get in step with them, and then we headed over to Georgia Avenue.

None of us knew what was going to happen next— whether Miss Summers would ever fall in love with Dad, whether both Marilyn and Crystal would give up on Lester, or whether I would really go the rest of seventh grade without making an enemy. But we were a family, and for right now, that was enough.

"The Three Musketeers, that's us," I said, beaming. Somebody was whistling again, I noticed, and it was Dad.

PHYLLIS REYNOLDS NAYLOR remembers seventh grade for her struggles with mathematics, the wall kick and the frog stand in gym, frying liver in home economics, and embarrassing herself on stage. As a mother, she has suffered through seventh grade with both of her sons, now grown, but enjoys going back to junior highs and middle schools to talk about her books and to see how things have changed.

About her Alice books, Phyllis Naylor says, "If I had known there would be a sequel to The Agony of Alice, and then another and another, I would have started Alice in the third grade." She plans to take Alice up to her eighteenth year before she stops the series, and already knows how the last book will end.

She lives in Bethesda, Maryland, with her husband, Rex, and is the author of sixty books, including The Agony of Alice; Alice in Rapture, Sort Of; Night Cry; The Solomon System; *and* The Keeper.